THE MORNING AFTER MOURNING

A Memoir

Starla Lipscomb

Published and Distributed By
The Lipscomb Publishing House
Phoenix, Arizona
Email: sbhoskins17@gmail.com

Packaging/Consulting
Professional Publishing House
1425 W. Manchester Ave. Ste B
Los Angeles, California 90047
323-750-3592
Email: professionalpublishinghouse@yahoo.com
www.professionalpublishinghouse.com

Cover design: TWASolutions.com
First printing October 2021
979-8-9850369-0-9
10987654321

To my mother, Vanessa Hutcherson.

Acknowledgments

I give glory to God as being the mastermind behind this book. He inspired every page and every word. I was simply the pen, but He was the ink and the hand that moved me. Without His unfailing love and guidance, this book wouldn't be possible. I didn't fully understand Your plan, but I'm thankful Your plan is always perfect and it worked in my favor. Thank You for picking me up, binding my wounds, and carrying me out of a dark and broken place. You gave me every ounce of strength I had to write this book with boldness, although at times it was very challenging. Thank you, Lord, for restoring my Sunday mornings. You are such an awesome God!

To my mother, the late Vanessa Hutcherson, I dedicate this book to you. Losing you was the hardest challenge I've ever faced, but I say thank you for preparing me to continue to live life even after you left this earth. Before leaving, you told me everything would be okay. You were right. The life lessons you taught me I still remember and practice to this day. I wish we could have had more time together, but I'm extremely grateful for the time we had. You are the strongest woman I know. Thank you for being such an amazing mother. I love you, Mama.

To my father, Charles Hoskins. Thank you for holding my hand through the difficult nights I faced. You've been there through every step and stage of my life. The nights of walking around the park and going for drives in the country just to talk about life left a deeper impression than you may know. As a young girl who needed her father, you were right there. I may have lost my mother, but I have a strong father who is there to stand by my side. I love you very much, Daddy.

To my stepmother, Linda Hoskins. There has never been a time in my life where you treated me like a stepdaughter, but as if I was your very own flesh and blood. You've loved me since day one, even before I lost my mother. I appreciate you so much. I love you, Linda.

To my husband, Arron Lipscomb Sr. Although you and I met years after losing my mother, you were a huge support in making certain I healed of my wounds. You're a huge advocate of communicating, counseling, forgiving, and teaching me the importance of getting back up after life has knocked you down. Thank you for being my support and thank you for being my best friend. I love you.

To my children, Vanessa and Arron Jr., please know that Mama loves you! Having you helped me to understand the pricelessness of motherhood. You two have been an unexplainable joy! I want you to know that for every dark day you may face, please remember that God will cause the sun to shine again. I'm excited to see what God has in store for you. I'm rooting for you all the way!

To my grandmother, Margaret Hoskins, and great aunts, Rosie Milligan, Clara King, and Owen Nelson. Thank you for pouring wisdom and knowledge into the next generation. All of you are Black women authors that inspire me to do and become the same. Thank you.

To my mentors/big brother and sisters, Keneisha Hoskins, Yolanda Bell, Lashonna Washington, Kesha Simmons, and Malik Rasheed. Thank you for being a ray of light in my life. The constant support you have given has been more life-changing than you know.

To my closest friends, Mariah, Jazmyn, Jasmine, Stephanie, Donneyale, and Brittany P. Thank you for being there. Every heartfelt moment we've shared has had a tremendous impact on me. Thank you for all the love and support over the years. I love y'all!

To all my other supportive relatives, church family, and families that have adopted me as their own, I say thank you. Your support helped get me to the place I am now in life. Whether you've known me from birth or later on down the years, thank you for being a part of my life.

> *"... weeping endureth for a night, but joy*
> *cometh in the morning."*
> –Psalm 30:5

Table of Contents

Webster's Dictionary defines **grief** as:
- Deep or poignant distress
- A result of suffering
- Trouble or annoyance
- An unfortunate outcome
- Mishap

"And God said, Let there be light."
– Genesis 1:3

God's Day

Every morning the sun rises. Even when there's cloud coverage, the sun is still present. When it rains, when it snows, and when there's fog, the sun still sits high in the sky. The sun, regardless of its position, can illuminate everything that is around it. Gracing everything living or inanimate by its rays.

When I was a child, the brilliance of the sun seemed greatest on Sunday mornings. To say the sun shines brightest on Sunday is far from a scientific fact, but my love for what's known as "God's Day" caused my eyes to see the Sunday morning sun in a more enlightening way than what I saw on any other day of the week. It was simply beautiful in every way. Sunday mornings consisted of getting up early and preparing to go to one of my favorite places: God's House, the church. Whether it was in the morning, afternoon, or evening, I adored entering God's House. The music, the people, the events, and the overall experience of the presence and power of God made the church more than just a building. It was a second home. In addition, Sunday was also the day of the week my family would gather on holidays, such as Easter, Mother's Day, Father's Day, graduations, and if a relative came into town to visit. With all this being said, the brilliance from the sun was just that more special on a Sunday, with so many heartfelt moments that took place on this day. From a natural perspective, I loved the Sunday morning sun so that I would even open my blinds slightly Saturday night before going to bed just so the Sunday morning sun woke me up as the warm rays beamed across my face. The gentle rays would let me know that my favorite day and time of the week had officially begun.

Sunday mornings were calm, and they were pleasant. They were easygoing, yet eventful.

However, there came a time in my life when even my beloved Sunday mornings were no longer peaceful and enjoyable. My happy mornings became mournful mornings. No longer did I wait in anticipation for the sun to rise on the following morning, once night came. Instead, I became oblivious to the beauty of the sun altogether. My pain and sorrow became cloud coverage. My sleepless nights became my rain. Day became night and night became midnight, as if the sun wasn't there at all. This was an unprecedented time in my life.

Years later, I can now testify that daybreak finally came. And Although the grief I carried seemed to consume and override any hope, I had to experience the joy of a Sunday morning again; I am glad to say that it wasn't able to.

To anyone who has ever suffered a loss, whether recently or in the past, expectedly or unexpectedly, I want to encourage you. The impact of grief is beyond what anyone could predict before going through it. The pain is immense and, at times, feels unbearable even when put upon the strongest of shoulders. But please understand that the scripture *"...joy cometh in the morning"* (Psalm 30:5) is ever so true.

I cannot provide you with an exact expiration date for your nighttime experience, but the same God who, with purpose, allows the sun to set, also holds the power to cause it to rise again. For even after experiencing heartbreak, pain, and grief you are more than able to experience a *Morning After Mourning*.

Keynon

The first funeral I remember attending was when I was five years old. The year being 1997.

Being so young, I wasn't exactly sure what was happening. However, despite my age, I remember vivid details of the funeral.

I entered a room that was full of chattering people. The colors were alarming to me. There was so much pink and orange. So many bright lights! Being only five years old, all I could see were the legs and feet of the adults above and around me. As I walked hand-in-hand with my mother, suddenly my uncle came beside me and lifted me onto his shoulders. It was then that I could see what the commotion was all about. While extended into the air, I looked into the center of the room to see a long coffin with someone I knew laying inside of it. I thought, *Keynon.*

The young man was my best friend's older brother. I had known and been around him all of my short life.

Quickly, my uncle put me back down on the floor, and just as he led me into the funeral room, I was moving closer to view the body. I just did not understand what was happening. As we got closer to the casket to view the body, I looked over to the right of the room to see someone else I knew. *Cathy*, I thought. It was the mother of both the deceased and my childhood best friend. She was sitting hunched over in a chair. She was crying so much! I had also known her all my life, and I had never seen her like this before. Her family surrounded her on each side in hopes to comfort her. Although, as a five-year-old, I could not verbally express what I felt, I knew this wasn't an ordinary day.

This sad day was over twenty years ago despite that, I remember the thoughts and feelings I experienced. Although this was my first encounter with death, it would not be my last. At a very tender age, the Lord allowed me to see a glimpse of death, using this moment to prepare me mentally and emotionally for the long road that was ahead.

"My voice shalt thou hear in the morning, O LORD; in the morning will I direct my prayer unto thee, and will look up."
– Psalm 5:3

Superwoman

Vanessa Hutcherson.

Daughter, sister, friend, caretaker, nurse, business owner, amongst other titles, but for me, she was Mama. The only one who could call her so. I was her only child. She was a piece of my sunshine and I hers. Relaxing on the couch, watching *Law & Order,* and traveling to different cities to see relatives and friends were some things we enjoyed doing together. Regarding personal hobbies, my mother loved to crotchet blankets and collect dolls, figurines, and black art.

My mother had a distinct aura about herself. She was very task and business-oriented. Life ran like clockwork when my mother was around; focused and not easily distracted. Business professional, but still very friendly. She didn't believe in wasting time, nor in being lazy. One of her key phrases was "Do what you have to do even when you're tired." In the eyes of my mother, hard work was the answer to everything. So much of who I am, I learned from her.

Mostly, my mother was a healthy woman. I honestly can't even recall a time where she suffered from even the flu or a common cold. She practically seemed invincible. However, during the fall of 2008, this aspect of her changed.

Being sixteen years old, my world centered on the typical concerns of a teenager: enjoying high school, working my first job, hanging with friends, latest trends, crushes, and overall preparing for college and adulthood. However, amongst these things, I'm glad to say my relationship with God was a focal point. I loved God and understood the importance of having a relationship with Him. My relationship with God was an anchor for me. During this time, I was still young in my faith and I still had much to learn.

"Yet the LORD will command his lovingkindness in the daytime, and in the night his song shall be with me, and my prayer unto the God of my life."
– Psalm 42:8

Unanswered Questions

One night, my mother suffered from immense pain in her abdomen area. She didn't complain much about it, but I remember seeing her hold her stomach tightly while sitting. Crouching over in pain as she slightly rocked back and forth. As I watched her, I was at a loss for words. I had never seen my mother like this before. She was never sick so I didn't understand what was happening. After suffering for hours and failing to manage the pain, a family member suggested she should go to the emergency room. At first, she refused, but thankfully, once the pain became unbearable, she obliged. On a fall night, she went to the hospital.

I can't give exact details as to the days following my mother coming home from the emergency room, but I definitely knew something was wrong. My mother wasn't the type to complain, nor easily shaken. Although she was very resilient, I knew something was bothering her. She was present physically, accomplishing her normal task as usual, but her eyes seemed distant and her voice weakened. I didn't know what was wrong or what had happened, but something definitely was wrong. I wanted to ask about that night when she was admitted to the emergency room, but how do you ask a woman that had always seemed invincible

"What's wrong?" So, I decided it was best to leave my questions unanswered.

Time went on and nothing was mentioned regarding my mother's health. It was as if the night in the emergency room had never happened. However, on the night of December 5, 2008, my father had come by our home to speak with my mother. For some time, they talked alone, but after a while, my father called me downstairs from my bedroom. He stated that he and my mother needed to speak with me. Not too concerned, but still wondering, I came downstairs inquisitive as to what was going on. Once I arrived downstairs, my mother and father were both sitting in the living room. The television was on and they both had been quietly talking as I entered the room. Things *seemed* normal mostly. I entered the living room and sat down in the armchair nearest the side of the couch where my mother sat. My father sat on the other end of the couch. Even though the television was on, the only sounds I remember hearing were the words from my parents, letting me know that my mother had recently been diagnosed with cancer. As expected, their faces showed worry and concern. Not only for the illness itself, but just as much for wondering how I would take such alarming news. It was obvious that my parents expected a reaction of tears and sorrow. Maybe even an emotional breakdown. On this night, though, this wasn't the case. I sat in the armchair and continued to let my parents speak, but in my mind, I already knew what my response would be. Still young in my faith, but having heard and witnessed the power of God in the lives of the saints around me, with all assurance, I simply told my parents, "You must not know the God I serve."

Upon hearing this unexpected response, their eyes widened, and, for a few moments, silence filled the room. There were no tears, nor a storming away from being overwhelmed with emotions. I continued to sit, yet my posture tall, in the living room armchair. It was settled: I was choosing to put my trust in God for my mother's health. My parents spoke more words to me, and not long after, they excused me to go back upstairs to my room. I entered my room, closed the door, and replayed the life-changing conversation that had just happened. I gathered my thoughts and prayed. I continued to say to myself, "I know God is gonna heal my mama."

In my heart, I knew everything would be okay.

"The LORD is my light and my salvation; whom shall I fear? the LORD is the strength of my life; of whom shall I be afraid?"
– Psalm 27:1

A Temporary Change

My hopes were high, and I invested my faith in God. It may seem extreme to some, but with the news I had received, I put my faith into action. Along with personal prayer and contacting a few of the saints, I also researched and found scriptures within the Word of God that spoke about physical and mental healing. Thereafter, I posted these scriptures on the walls of our home. It was an act of faith that some didn't understand, but I knew it would have a positive effect on all who saw and read them. Especially my mother. There is immense power in reading and rehearsing God's Word, which births faith within us. His Word is the foundation of our faith.

"So then faith cometh by hearing, and hearing by the word of God." (Romans 10:17) The more we hear, receive, and apply God's Word, the more our faith will grow. With the challenge we were facing, faith was essential. I was a teenager, but my understanding and love for God began at a very young age. My beloved grandmothers spooned-fed me the Word of God. Mrs. Margaret Hoskins and Mrs. Georgetta Lewis. I'm very grateful that God used them as an avenue to bring me to Him. So, once I became a teenager, God's Word had taken deep root in my life. I may not have understood why God allowed my mother to be sick, but I trusted Him to save and deliver her from the illness. For years, I heard and witnessed the testimonies of the saints

about how mighty God was. I had read the scriptures for myself. I knew it to be true! Now it was time for another testimony to be birthed. Cancer was a small issue for God to handle. He had proven Himself before and I knew He could again.

I was my mother's only child. However, living in our home at the onset of her illness was my mother, a younger cousin, and me. For some time, things remained normal and our home continued to run like clockwork, as it always had. But in time, my mother's illness limited her energy and mobility. Not only was our home affected, but her careers were, too. It was decided that it was better for her to leave her occupations and remain at home, where she could rest and focus on her health and wellbeing. With this decision, my mother never complained about this needed change, but for someone that lived by the motto of hard work and fulfilled so many notable roles, this new way of life wasn't necessarily easy. She understood it had to be done. We all did. For me, I was an active student halfway through my junior year, and greatly involved in extracurricular activities at school and my local church, as well as being a part-time employee at my first job at the movie theater. I maintained these responsibilities while also maintaining the housekeeping duties and also tending to my younger cousin that lived with us. With so much to balance, it wasn't long before we needed additional assistance. Our circumstances were becoming taxing.

After New Year's 2009, one of my mother's sisters came and moved in with us. She cooked, washed, and helped fulfill the housekeeping duties we needed help with. With this needed help, life was balancing again with our normal day-to-day tasks. Even with the accepted new changes, my hope was still greatly invested in returning to our former way of life: my mother resuming her role as superwoman while I continued to enjoy my remaining high school years. My faith and thoughts remained the same. Even with the new changes, *Mama will be healed, after a while. This change is only temporary.*

A Window of Hope

In the blink of an eye, the dreary winter was passing, and spring was drawing near. Finally, the sunshine was coming back! Although the summer of my senior year was still a few months away, I almost couldn't contain my excitement. I was excited to take my class photo, spend time with friends, and get ready for my freshman year of college. I had much to look forward to. I had worked hard during my high school years as I prepared myself for college and adulthood. I was excited to begin this new season in my life. However, my excitement for the upcoming year was short-lived and overshadowed as my mother's health drastically changed.

In spring 2009, Provena Hospital became our second home. Not because my mother returned to her occupation of being a nurse, but because her health waned. In contrast to the current circumstances, I once loved visiting the hospital. As a child, being able to visit the hospital with my mom was absolutely exciting. Saying hello to her coworkers, walking down the long hallways, and riding the elevators was thrilling to me! My visits with her to the hospital now were drastically different. I wasn't a child anymore and my mother wasn't that same invincible nurse anymore. The long hallways that I once skipped happily through were now cold and intimidating. The innocent eagerness I once had for being able to push the elevator button was no longer exciting. I dreaded it, knowing the ride up was taking me to see someone I loved so much suffer from an illness. The hospital was no longer a fun place. To be honest, I hated it.

As I would step out of the elevator onto the hospital floor, there were days I would intentionally take a hallway detour before entering my mother's room. When doing this, I would take a moment to stop and gaze out of a hallway window. There was nothing, in particular, I wanted to see, but I would purposely use this moment to take a few minutes to enjoy the sight and warmth of the sun. It was a comfort to me. Reminding me of my beloved Sunday mornings, a time I was hopeful for again. While looking out of the hall window, my mind would refuge in a place far away. And with this, for a moment, life was normal again. It was as if I was no longer standing in a hospital hallway, but somewhere I actually wanted to be. But, after a while, I knew I had to face my reality. So, I would once again continue my walk down the hall to my mother's room.

This is temporary. She'll be home soon, I would say to myself.

Invisible Tears

Painstakingly, as the weeks passed during spring 2009, my mother's admittance into the hospital became a revolving door. Being released and sent home only to be admitted back a week or two later. It was physically and mentally exhausting. Especially for my mother.

When visiting her, I would consciously brace myself before entering her room. I would take a moment and have a mental conversation with myself: *Starr, hold it together. Pull back those tears. There's no reason to cry. God is going to heal her. Remember what the Word says. Watch TV and talk to her just like you would, as if you were home. Keep yourself together.* I made certain to do exactly that. Externally, I was composed, but inwardly I was completely overwhelmed.

As time went on and the hospital stays became more frequent, it was hard to admit, but my faith was wavering. I was growing weary. To be honest, I was disappointed in myself. I asked myself, *Why do I feel this way? Where is my faith? Pull it together Starr.* My mind was swamped with a thousand thoughts.

Seeing my invincible mother's health slowly deteriorate right before my eyes was heartbreaking, to say the least. It caused a deep inward sorrow that initially I was unaware that I carried inside of me. Week after week of witnessing my mother's condition, I quickly realized that cancer is a merciless disease.

It is a disease that completely takes over the body. Because of the cancer, I witnessed my mother lose weight rapidly. She lost weight to where her skeleton showed through her weakened skin on every area of her body. Her average full-size figure dropped to be under one hundred pounds. The illness, as expected, caused her to lose physical strength, too. There were times while walking that she would fall to the floor because she could not maintain herself and her extremities. Thus, ultimately causing her to depend on a walker. Besides the cancer itself, the medications had very overpowering effects. Causing her to be semi-conscious and unable to have a normal conversation. She would muster up as much strength as she could to move and speak, but the medications would, most times, win. There was just so much to this illness! The vomiting, the bedpans, the shallow breathing, the rigidness of her frail body, the adult diapers, the medication, the tubes and IVs, and the horrid constant beeping sounds from the hospital machines only added to the misery. I can vividly recall it all. The images are embedded in my mind beyond my control. It got to a point that I had night terrors.

It became extremely overwhelming and too much for me to take. It felt like my head was spinning. As one of her primary caretakers, sometimes I felt the need to escape. Even if only to my room. There were many times I would simply seclude myself in my room, slump against a wall, and stare off into the distance, wondering when it would all end.

When will God finally heal my mother?

Night had taken its toll, and I was ready for morning.

Although I was worn, I'm grateful I wasn't alone. During this distressing time of my life, the Lord sent and also led me to people that encouraged me. People that knew my story and received me with open arms. With the great support I had, my father was the greatest. My father made certain to make sure that I was taken care of and mentally and emotionally stable during this critical time. This being something he had always done, but now it was even more so. Daily calls and check-ins were the norm and added to this, my father always made certain to take me out for dinner periodically, take night walks around the park, and do anything else he could for daddy-daughter quality time. My most beloved time of bonding was our long drives into the country. We were headed to no set destination or location. Instead, it was a time that my father would intentionally plan out so I could have a mental rest from my heartache. Something he knew I desperately needed.

Our country drives were long and purposeful. As we drove around, our conversations ranged from serious talks about life and the journey thereof to movies we had recently watched to playful sarcasm and anything else in between. Nearing sunset is when our drives would take place. It was awesome to see the green country fields graced by a touch from the sun. When looking up, the idle clouds only added to the beauty. I cherished these moments with my father. I cherished these moments of seeing God's beautiful creation. These moments were unforgettable.

Choice Words

It wasn't long before others, outside of our family, heard and knew of my mother's illness. Being a part of a small community like that of Danville, Illinois, it doesn't take long for news to travel. Our household received familiar and even unfamiliar visitors.

Relatives came to visit from out of town and phone calls and greeting cards frequently came to our house. With the traffic that was coming in and out, I took the time to sit back and observe how people responded to seeing and being around my mother with her illness. I observed a lot. I watched as some visitors were completely normal and held pleasant conversations with my mother as if nothing was wrong. I admired that. Some would welcome themselves to the kitchen and bring meals and prepare dishes for us to eat. That was nice to see too. And also some visitors would awkwardly sit and only make semi eye contact with my mother. Not for lack of respect, but because they were unsure of how to behave. Being there was difficult for them. Which I understood completely. Seeing your loved one sick can be overwhelming. And then others were expected to come by, but never came. This wasn't easy to witness. I can't say whether this hurt my mother, but it definitely hurt me. I didn't understand the absence. I didn't understand how they were present when my mother was strong and healthy, but when severely sick, they weren't. But this became a life-changing learning opportunity for me. Just from these simple observations I came to realize and understand the complexity of people. Everyone responds differently to not only sickness, but any challenging circumstance. I had to humbly view things from a different perspective. I had to accept that it wasn't an issue of whether the absent people loved my mother or not, but more so whether they truly had the strength to handle seeing a loved one in such a strenuous condition. I had to consider and ponder these questions: *Would visiting my mother be a painful reminder of a loved one they lost previously? Did they not want to be an inconvenience to my mother, with so many other visitors coming by? Did they even know my mother was as desperately ill as she was? Did they think cancer was contagious?* Either way, this experience taught me to be grateful for those that were present during this time and to show no disdain for the ones that weren't. The important thing is that my mother was greatly loved. Loved by many down here on earth and even more so loved by God who sat high in the heavens. That's what mattered most.

As plenty of visitors continued to come to our home, I was also greeted by friends, teachers, co-workers and fellow church members when out in public. Numerous people would approach me asking about my mother's condition and how my mother was doing. These encounters were expected, but still something that was difficult to handle. When speaking, I'd never give full details about the unpleasant side of the illness, but instead would mention things such as if she had an increased appetite or if she was recently released from the hospital. I would provide them information on the positive side of things. Inwardly I fought and refused to allow or give anyone a reason to feel sorry for me or my mother. Just as I did since the beginning, I would constantly rehearse in my mind: *It's okay. God is going to heal her.* Once the conversations would come to a close, the person would usually sum it up by stating that they would continue to pray for her. I would respond and tell them thank you. It was always very relieving when these conversations were over. These encounters mostly were normal and received well although difficult to have. However, as time went on, I unexpectedly encountered conversations that weren't as encouraging. Horrifically, I encountered conversations and statements such as *Oh Starla! I heard your mom was dying. I'm so sorry.* With mentioning this statement alone, I'm sure you can imagine the confusion, hurt, and fury that ignited inside of me upon hearing these remarks. I thought to myself *Who in the world is spreading news that my mother is dying?? Did they just say that??* I would walk away feeling extremely offended and embarrassed.

Completely heartbroken as to the comments that were made. In my mind, anyone that thought or spoke in this way regarding my mother's illness was considered just as harmful as the cancer itself. Like drifting dark clouds overshadowing the sun, in my mind, these individuals were intentionally coming to block any and all light from shining down on us. *How dare they?* I thought to myself. After experiencing encounters such as this multiple times I made a conscious decision to become calloused towards people. I would allow them to speak to me regarding my mother, but I would limit the information given completely. The conversations became short and factual. Rigid and non-intimate. Other than those that were close friends or direct family I made the decision that anyone else didn't deserve to know anything about my mother's progress or condition. I just didn't understand. *Why were people giving up on my mother?*

Didn't they have faith like I did? She still has a chance! God would have the final say! Things may have looked bad and my feelings were hurt, but I refused to believe that my mother wouldn't be healed. And only a few weeks later, my faith in my mother's healing increased even more.

It was a day I will never forget.

A Ray of Healing

I cannot recall the exact date, but I remember my mother had been admitted into the hospital again and I was on my way to go and see her. As I approached the room I walked in to unexpectedly see my mother fully sitting up in the bed eating a meal.

Oh! I was astonished and filled with joy to see her in such a good condition. This was astonishing to me because her appetite was something that she had greatly struggled with for months. She even looked better! Her demeanor was different! The day or so before a friend and local pastor had come and laid hands on my mother to pray for her. And I was glad that he had come. I was immediately reminded of the scriptures that states *Is any sick among you? let him call for the elders of the church; and let them pray over him, anointing him with oil in the name of the Lord: And the prayer of faith shall save the sick, and the Lord shall raise him up;...* (James 5:14-15) God had heard our prayers and was executing a wonder right before our eyes. Her appetite had returned and her vitals were at great levels.

Soon the cancer would be gone and we would soon return to our normal lives.

God, thank you.

The Art of Suppression

Just as quickly as the forecast changes, so did our circumstances. Not long after my mother had made such great progress with her health and had come home, she was once again readmitted back to the hospital. This alone tore me apart, but in addition, my father's health became a concern. While visiting my mother, I received a phone call letting me know that my father was downstairs in the very same hospital in the E.R. *Is this really happening?? Lord please no.*

As I got up to leave the room to rush downstairs, I couldn't understand what was taking place.

God, I can't take all this.

I didn't know what was exactly going on, but upon entering the emergency room, I saw my father sitting up on a stretcher as nurses checked his vitals and levels. My stepmother was there with him. I won't disclose the cause for his admittance into the E.R., but thankfully my father was released that same night. I was extremely relieved that my father was doing better. However, for myself, I was shaken to the core. I didn't realize it but it was during this moment that I learned the art of suppression. Suppression referring to the behavior of mentally removing and or blocking undesirable thoughts and feelings. Overall, suppression is a coping mechanism.

The idea of possibly having two ill parents was beyond strenuous in my heart and mind. Once things were checked and cleared, I said goodbye to my father and stepmother and returned upstairs to my mother.

Keep it together, Starr. This isn't the time to fall apart.

I stepped into the elevator and headed to my mother's room.

*"Let I pray thee, thy merciful kindness be for my comfort, according
to thy word unto thy servant."*
– Psalm 119:76

Cloud Coverage

*Starr, Carolyn passed away this week. She had a heart attack. They
found her.* My mother's eyes were distant and her voice small as
she relayed the news that her best friend of over thirty years had
passed away. My mother's closest friend, as well as my godmother.

Oh…

I wasn't sure how to respond. As I looked at my mother, her
demeanor was the same as the night after she had returned from
the E.R. It was obvious that her mind was riddled with thoughts,
but she wasn't willing or ready to reveal any of them. Her heart
was heavy and this, of course, was beyond understanding. The
same was true for me. I stood in shock as I heard the unfortunate
fate of my godmother.

Silence filled the room.

And although no tears were externally shed, without question,
my mother and I both had begun to grieve. Our pain wasn't
verbalized, but we both understood what the other was feeling.
The heaviness could be felt within the room. Some things in life
don't have to be said or explained. You just intuitively know. I
knew my mother, and she knew me.

We changed the topic and continued to converse about other
things.

I miss you, Carolyn.

That's as much as my mind and heart could handle to think.

Summer Awaits

June 1, 2009: My seventeenth birthday. This day was somewhat exciting, but of course, my mind was clouded with so many other things that my birthday was the least of my concerns. A few weeks prior to my birthday many changes had taken place. My younger cousin that lived with my mother and I had officially moved back to Indiana with his mother. He had lived with my mother and I for three years. I was going to miss him. In addition, school had ended and summer break had officially begun. My senior summer was here and my summer schedule would mainly comprise working at my job, hanging with friends, and being involved in events held at my church. Regarding my birthday, I had plans to hang with friends the night of, but during the afternoon I had plans to spend time with my mother at the hospital. Of course, the hospital wasn't necessarily where I imagined celebrating a birthday, but I was just happy to be around my parents and family.

That's all I really wanted for my birthday. Outside of myself and my father, collectively there were about six people, family members, that were there visiting her that day as well. Photos were taken of us all and I was told there was cake and ice cream waiting at home for me. My mother may not have been able to join us, but my father made sure that he made my birthday special. I appreciated that.

*"Truly the light is sweet, and a pleasant thing it is
for the eyes to behold the sun."*
– Ecclesiastes 11:7

Pleasant Surprise

As I mentioned before, one of the many reasons Sundays was such a joyous time was because on the holidays that fell on a Sunday, such as Easter, Mother's Day, Father's Day, and Christmas, I would wake up to not only the sun beaming through the window but also the sound of pots and pans being filled with food downstairs in the kitchen. While the wonderful smell of soul food wafted upstairs to my room. On holidays my mother and her sisters would each prepare a dish and then collectively meet at our home around a set time. Our home was the designated home to celebrate the holidays. This was a tradition that existed for years. This tradition continued and remained even during my mother's illness. June 21 was the date of Father's Day 2009. I expected my family to arrive that Sunday afternoon. However, on June 20 I arrived home from work and was greeted by a house full of family members. This was completely unexpected. *Why is everyone here today instead of tomorrow?* I wondered to myself. I wasn't certain why they were at our home on Saturday instead of the next day Sunday, but I was happy for them to be there, regardless. There were family members talking at the kitchen table, watching TV in the living room, and anywhere else there was seating. Enjoying one another's company just as we would on any given holiday. Our family sat and chatted in every room except the sun room.

In our home, adjacent to the living room was what we referred to as the "sun room."

It was like that of a living room, but smaller. This room housed a television, family photos, a white radiator, and of course windows. 3 sets of windows. It was by far the brightest room in our home. It was typically used as a lounge area or for overflow when guests were over. But within the last few months, it was transformed into my mother's bedroom. The couch was removed and a hospital bed was put in its place. Everything else in the room remained the same. Although my mother was always home, she still enjoyed moving to different areas around the house. So, when I arrived home she was sitting in the kitchen with the family. It was great to see everyone talking and spending time with one another. As the day drew on and the family began to go home for the evening giving their goodbyes, my mother relocated back to her bedroom. It was time to get ready for Sunday morning.

Sunday

Sunday morning! Sunday was here, and the sun was definitely out! It was a hot summer day. No rain, no dark overcast, no fog. It was my perfect kind of day. As always, I got up and began to get myself ready for church. My mother had been absent from church for a while now by this point for understandable reasons. Our home was only five minutes away from the church. I had my own car so getting myself ready on a Sunday morning was unrushed. This Sunday however was a holiday and unlike other holidays no food was being cooked downstairs. And with this, I assumed that no relatives were coming by since they came just the day before. I could tell this Sunday would be a nontraditional holiday, but I didn't mind. My mother needed her rest. I didn't have to go to work that evening so my plans for the day were simple: Go to the Sunday services and then come home and be with my mama. *This is going to be a good day.*

I arrived home from church service around 1:45 p.m. Surprisingly another aunt, one of my mother's sisters that lived out of town, came to stay the night. So, there were four of us in our home for the evening. I came home, changed clothes, and went to tend to my mother. But when checking in on her I automatically knew something wasn't right. My mother was still lying in her bed as she had the night before.

Startled, I asked my aunt if there was something wrong. My aunt responded simply *Your mother can't walk anymore.*

Silence.

Immediately I began to panic in my mind. My lips were still, but my mind was going haywire.

What do you mean CAN'T walk anymore?

She was just fine yesterday?

What?? Is that even possible??

I physically kept myself composed, but mentally I forced myself to go into my safe place as I had done so many times before. *It's okay. God is going to heal her. God is going to heal her. God is going to heal her. It's okay… It will all be okay. Keep it together Starr.*

As I gazed at my mother I quickly realized that she also hadn't said a word the entire time. She was there, but at the time she wasn't there. I realized now more than ever she needed me as her daughter to be by her side. So that night I decided to sleep downstairs with my mother in her bedroom. I made a pallet of blankets and grabbed a pillow to lie down with. I made myself as comfortable as I could. I knew it would be a while before I finally fell asleep.

The night drew on and my aunts came in and out to check on her periodically. It wasn't long before I grew tired and soon prepared myself for bed. It had been a long day. I adjusted myself on the floor with my pallet, turned the television off, and went to sleep. I was ready for Monday morning. My Sunday had proven to be less spectacular than I imagined.

"O send out thy light and thy truth: let them lead me..."
– Psalm 43:3

The Beloved Sunroom

I was awakened out of my sleep on Monday morning to a knock on the front porch door. It was about 9:30 am. *Who could that be?* I thought.

I wasn't told that we'd have any visitors coming by so I was curious who was knocking at our door. I got up off my pallet on the floor and looked over at my mother. She seemed the same as the night before. Present, yet not present. I shook myself free from my thoughts and went to answer the door. It was Cathy. Our good family friend and also the woman who lost her son several years before. Like my mother, she was also a nurse. They worked together. This wasn't the first visit she had made over the months so I thought little of it when she came. Unexpected or not, she was someone that was always welcome. I opened the door and welcomed her in. We spoke a few words and then she sat with my mother in the sun room. I figured it was best that I didn't return to my floor pallet, but instead go upstairs to continue sleeping. Exhausted, I passed out on the bed and dozed off to sleep.

Approximately 30 minutes passed before I was once again awakened out of my sleep.

Starr... Starr...

Half asleep I figured I was hearing things. The voice wasn't really audible. So, I continued to sleep assuming my exhaustion was getting the best of me. But the voice became louder and louder followed by footsteps coming up the stairs.

Starr...

However, I quickly realized I wasn't imagining things at all.

My aunt came into my room and before I could fully wake up she completely lost her composure.

"She done took that last breath! She gone, Starr! Ya mama gone!"

Immediately my grogginess left and in full strength, I sprinted downstairs.

I ran down the flight of stairs.

What do you mean gone??

I pushed past the table and chairs in the kitchen.

Gone as in passed away?

I ran through the dining room.

No, that's impossible. I was JUST with her.

I ran through the living room. "

This can't be happening...

I came into the sun room.

When I finally made it to the sun room, I made it just in time to see my mother fall forward in a slump and caught in the hands and arms of Cathy. As just like the trained professional nurse she was, she gently laid my mother down for her final rest.

Silence.

It's as if the ground beneath completely vanished. I didn't know where I was.

I didn't know who I was.

My life had completely stopped.

To be honest, at that very moment it felt as though something on the inside of me died along with my mother.

"Go ahead and call your daddy." My aunt's words caused me to snap back into reality.

My aunt handed me the house phone. I tried to dial the number, but couldn't. I had to leave.

Without so much as getting dressed, washing, or anything else, I immediately grabbed my car keys and jumped in my car. Like a dazed maniac, I sped over to my father's house. Whether I had my seatbelt on I don't know. I can't even recall if I actually stopped at the traffic signs. All I know is that I arrived alive and in one piece to my father and stepmother's home with the most devastating news I've ever had to relay. Like my aunt, I ran upstairs out of breath calling their name. "Linda! Daddy! LINDA! DADDY!"

I stumbled up the stairs crawling trying to make it to the top. I had no strength left within me. It felt as though my body had completely shut down. Upon hearing my voice my stepmother appeared from around the corner and reached out to me with her arms. With little strength to speak, I spoke as audibly as I could: "She's……. gone."

My stepmother helped me up the stairs. Completely weak, I was unable to say anything else. I walked into the bedroom to see my father sitting on the edge of the bed near the window. His face was stark and rigid. He already knew.

I fell to his side and sat down next to him on the bed. I couldn't breathe.

I couldn't even fully think.

And after months of forcing myself to keep it together, it was at that moment that I completely lost it. All the pain, disappointment, confusion, and overall grief convulsed through my body and completely broke me apart. Like shattered glass, it felt as though I had been smashed and broken into a million pieces. My emotions were everywhere and I couldn't control them. My father remained silent and simply pulled me into his arms. We continued to sit on the edge of the bed near the window for some time. The window was open, and the sun was bright. But at that moment the shine and warmth of the sun didn't matter. It didn't matter at all.

– Psalm 143:8

An Unopened Letter

"Now Starla, I need you to be strong." My grandmother eased her way out of her bedroom with her walker and sat down across from me on the couch. It was about 8:00 a.m., Tuesday morning. The day following my mother's death.

"Be strong…" Her words stung. *I don't want to be strong.* I thought to myself. My grandmother, more than anyone else, understood the pain I felt from losing my mother. She too had also lost her mother at seventeen years old. Although this occurred over fifty years prior, my grandmother could still vividly recall what she saw and felt the day her mother died. Her words to me may have been difficult to hear, but I understood it was coming from an intimate place. My grandmother loved me and had personally taken this time to teach me that *"being strong"* was more than possible. And that from this point forward in my life it was in fact a necessity. Her words stung, but she understood I needed to hear them. As she continued to talk, I sat and sobbed unsure of what to say in response. "I thought God was going to heal her," was what I was able to muster up and say before breaking down again. In calmness, she reassured me that everything would be alright in time. Giving me words of encouragement and comfort for me to remember. Once our conversation had ended, I returned to the guest bedroom and grabbed a notepad and pen, and began to write. It was time to come to terms with the life-changing experience I had just had. Writing has always been an outlet for me, allowing me to sit and collect my thoughts. As I sat, I began to write from the deepest place within my heart. Stopping from time to time to wipe my tears, but then continuing until I was complete. I knew that my mother would never read my poem, but I knew it would serve its purpose as a final goodbye letter from me to her.

My mother was gone, and although extremely painful, it was something I had to learn to accept.

I just didn't know how.

Expect the Unexpected

The week of my mother's funeral, as expected, was busy and overwhelming. Monday, June 22 to Saturday, June 27, without question, was the longest five days of my life. My appetite was nonexistent and sleep was scarce. It was only by the hand of God that I was able to continue to function fully day in and day out without fainting or collapsing. It was as if my mind had been programmed to autopilot for the entire week. Contacting family members, creating a program, moving into my father and stepmother's home and the dreadful task of having to pick my mother's coffin and tombstone was mind-blowing. *How is this my life now?* I continued to ask myself over and over. Within one day my life had completely changed. Having to walk into the same funeral parlor that I stood in years ago as a naïve five-year-old holding her mother's hand, made me realize how temporary life is. I was no longer a naïve child and my mother, the one who once held my hand, was now the person that everyone was coming to see and pay their respect to. *How is this happening?* I just couldn't understand.

In the past, when close family members had passed, like my grandparents, it was my mother who had the role in orchestrating the funerals. But now it was my turn to do so for her. *How in the world did she do all this over and over? This is emotionally exhausting.*

However, with this being said, I'm very grateful that my parents were there to help me with everything. Once again, my support system had my back.

The long, yet short week of my mother's death had flown by and it was now time for the services. I sat on the front row next to my father.

Teary-eyed and silent, I shook hand after hand of the many people that walked down the aisle to give me their condolences. As the services began, songs were sung, and the pulpit was graced by various friends and ministers that had words to share. Having cried constantly for the last week, I was mentally and emotionally exhausted. And as I stood up to walk to the casket to say my final goodbye to my mother, for a moment my life stopped again. But this time I understood what was going on. *This is my life now...* These were my raw thoughts as I pondered what life would be like now. I was numb, yet completely aware of my surroundings at the same time. My father grabbed me and hugged me tight and led me back to my seat.

This is my life now…

The service continued and soon it was time for the eulogy to be given. The speaker preached the message "Expect the Unexpected". It's almost as if he had read my mind. The sermon title described my personal thoughts and feelings perfectly. Like the typical funeral sermon, it was a message that encouraged the living to prepare themselves now for when their lives would end later. Knowing that eventually we all would have to stand before God one day.

After the service, the procession headed to the graveyard and then back to the church fellowship hall for the repast. I tried to eat, but was unable to. I was glad to see so many of my family and friends, but still the occasion overrode my joy of chatting and visiting with them. I composed myself as best as I could as the crowd continued to speak and greet me.

This is my life now…

"My soul waiteth for the Lord more than they that watch for the morning: I say, more than they that watch for the morning."
– Psalm 130:6

Decision After Decision

The next day was Sunday. Reflecting on the Sunday and the events thereof exactly one week prior, my spirit was heavy. However, as I had always done, I rose early and attended Sunday Morning service. It felt odd no longer having to wake up and tend to my mother. But I knew I had to continue living my life as normal as I could. As expected, upon arriving at church, I was approached and given condolences and words of encouragement for my loss. Having been a member of the church for seven years, the journey of my mother's illness was witnessed by the other members. Many of the saints stayed in contact, prayed, made hospital visits and went above and beyond to support us as a family. I was grateful for the love that was shown.

However, as the months passed by I made a personal decision to start a new membership at another local church. I had remained prayerful about this choice and decision and knew that God was before me. Prior to leaving, I had an open discussion with the Pastor and his wife letting both of them know about my decision to leave. When openly speaking to them they both understood my decision and let me know they loved and appreciated me. So, with a thank you and farewell I began my membership at another local church and continued to serve God. Although I initially felt spiritually strong and balanced after my mother's passing, I did not know that I would find myself in the greatest spiritual battle of my life.

"He hath led me, and brought me into darkness, but
not into light."
– Lamentations 3:2

Mourning for Mornings

"Saints of God, faith is the key! When ya' sick in ya body it's faith
that will bring healing! Amen and Amen! Our God is a healer!"

As I sat in the church pews on Sunday mornings, my ears would hear the sermons preached and my eyes would read the scripture text, but my heart was conflicted.

Was God really a healer? I silently asked these questions while allowing my thoughts to distract me from the preached message as I replayed my mother's death repeatedly in my mind. Never daring to speak my thoughts aloud, but keeping them buried deep down inside of me. It wasn't every Sunday that the sermon topic focused on healing, but when they did, it would always prick wounds that had yet to heal. I was still greatly unsettled regarding my mother's death.

As the preacher continued to preach and the crowd applauded and shouted amen, I remained submerged in my thoughts. It was as if I wasn't present in the Sunday service at all. The voice of the preacher was completely drowned out by my silent, yet loud thoughts.

Somebody say faith!

Did I not pray hard enough...?

The woman with the issue of blood, she believed!

But I did everything the scriptures told me to do…
According to your faith be it done unto you!
I had to watch her die…
He can do it in the midnight hour!
He healed other people, why not her…?
There's nothing that our God can't do!
I prayed and fasted for nothing…
Tell the Lord thank you for your healing!
The prayers didn't matter. God let her die anyway.

As I sat completely consumed in my thoughts, before I knew it, it was time for the altar call and final prayer. Sundays such as this became common for me. I would enter the church broken hearted and leave the same. Entering through the church doors with a false smile and a Praise the Lord greeting to the saints, yet bitter deep down on the inside. In service, I would robotically wave my hand saying "hallelujah" when prompted by the worship leader and I would attempt to sing a joyful tune as the congregational songs were sung. Physically I was present, yet mentally and emotionally I was absent. Sunday mornings were drastically different now. My beloved Sunday Mornings in God's House no longer brought me joy as it once did. I felt empty on the inside. The music no longer filled me and the people no longer gave me cheer. The warmth and fullness of God's House now felt empty and cold. Visually, I could see the presence of God moving within the service, but physically I didn't feel a part of it. Despite my attendance, deep down I no longer viewed God in the same light as I once did. The adamancy I once had for the scriptures and the conviction I had for believing in the power of prayer was no longer the same. Simply, my feelings were awkward and difficult to describe. Overall, I still loved God, but deep down I was betwixt. A part of me wanted to accept my mother's death as being God's Will, while another side of me felt as though God had abandoned me when I needed Him most.

I was in spiritual turmoil and I had no peace whatsoever. And as I would reminisce on my final days with my mother (family members coming to our home, my aunt choosing to stay the night prior, our family friend coming unexpectedly the morning of), I realized that these visits were made to be a last goodbye from our loved ones.

Secretly, yet openly, everyone knew that my mother's death was drawing near.

Everyone except me.

God how could you do that to me? I thought. I was entangled in feelings of confusion, disappointment, anger and resentment. No matter how hard I tried I just couldn't make sense of it all. Being overwhelmed with emotions, I didn't know what to think or feel. Was it wrong to have these feelings? Has anyone else ever felt this way?

Does God even still care? Should I even still care? I had no answers. I had never been in this place spiritually before and it was an extremely difficult challenge for me. I felt hollow on the inside. My mornings were now sunless.

I was at a standstill. I didn't want to backslide and abandon my faith and walk with God, but I also no longer wanted to give God my full trust again.

My spiritual life became altered:

When praying, I prayed in doubt.

When reading scriptures, I read with bitterness.

As I continued to serve God in various roles and positions, it was done more so out of obligation rather than from a place of worship and deep heartfelt desire. It was as if a dark cloud was permanently positioned over my head.

And due to my shame and hurt, I purposely hid my innermost feelings from others. I displayed a false image that I was spiritually valiant and unmoved in my faith despite my circumstances, but deep down my zeal for God had lost its potency. Personally, I felt like my prayers and faith in God had been in vain seeing that my greatest prayer, my mother being healed, didn't happen.

She was gone.

And there was no Sunday morning, regardless of how bright, that would be able to change that.

Life had lost its brilliance.

My mornings had been traded in for mourning.

Composed Insanity

Things were dark.

Everything seemed to make me angry, sad or frustrated. *What is going on with me?* I would think to myself.

I couldn't explain why I was so emotionally volatile. I would experience moments of happiness when suddenly I would have an emotional outburst and a complete breakdown. In addition to this volatility, I began to suffer from anxiety. (**Anxiety being defined as restlessness, worry or fear that directly affects a person's ability to be able to healthfully function in their daily activities.**)

I was swarming with unsettled emotions connected to my mother's death and other circumstances, and I remained on edge and easily triggered by anything that reminded me of the loss. It was a constant whirlwind of emotions that seemed unstoppable. The Sunday mornings I once had were nonexistent. I would wake up feeling overwhelmed with anxiety. Worrying and feeling uneasy about my set plans for the day. Pondering and imagining possibilities that weren't typical for me to think.

What if something terrible happens today? What if I DIED today? I thought.

I would feel anxiety over every major and minor matter. Matters as simple as the weather forecast to major issues such as whether I could possibly die that day unexpectedly.

I suffered torment during the day and also at night. Even while asleep, a time when rest is expected, I would experience nightmares. I was terrorized to a point that I began sleeping in the bed with my parents for a while. The night was absolutely frightening to me. The dark shadows and stillness made me extremely uncomfortable and nervous. It reminded me of death in every way. Every sound and unexplainable noise made me paranoid. To be honest, I felt as though I was on the verge of a mental breakdown. While suffering with the paranoia, I questioned if the shadows and unexplainable noises I heard at night were my mother.

I think I'm going insane. This can't be happening. I think I'm going crazy. Reasoning back and forth within myself, I came to the conclusion that losing my mother was slowly destroying my life.

Overall, whether awake or asleep I had no peace. I was completely suffocated by fear and anxiety.

Even with this being said, ironically, I would receive accolades from loved ones about how well I seemed to be managing the loss of my mother. Statements such as *Wow, Starr you're so strong. You're handling it all so well. I don't know what I'd do if I were in your predicament.* were made often. Knowing that these comments were coming from a sincere, yet naïve place, in response I would give the typical "thank you." Allowing the person to assume that in fact their observation was valid when in reality it was anything but. Suppressed in my mind was a voice that was screaming for help. But even still, I chose to stay silent.

In an attempt to cope, I tried to find solace in the things that once brought me joy. For example, the holidays were one of the most enjoyable times for me as a child. During the holidays I made an effort to become excited and surround myself with loved ones. Visiting the homes of multiple relatives and spending countless hours catching up on anything new. But sadly, my attempt was futile. Regardless of the season or the holiday occasion I still found little joy. Yes, my family was present and the beloved soul food was too, but my mother wasn't. Holidays were no longer the same. And this fact was undeniable.

With the appetite that I had, if any, I would eat. And I would continue to include myself in the laughs and conversations, but the void I felt wouldn't leave. I was very grateful to be in the midst of family, but I wasn't happy. From my personal perspective the holidays were an enjoyable time for those around me, but for me they were miserable.

Seeking solace still, there were days that I would randomly get into my car and go for a drive around town. When driving, I would intentionally drive past my childhood home. The home where my mother and I lived: 1129 N. Walnut Street.

A beautiful two story brick house that was our home for fifteen years. Countless memories were made in that home. I missed it dearly. After the morning that my mother passed away, I never went back to stay. I had no desire to live there thereafter. It was sold and a new family now occupied it. This too was difficult to come to terms with.

As I approached the street while driving, I would have flashbacks to my former life. *I just want to see my home again. I can't go back, but seeing it should make me feel better.*

With this in mind, I would ease my way down the street and linger before the house. It looked perfectly the same: The tall tree sat to the left of the porch and a long gravel driveway wound its way to the back of the house to the garage. The front porch wood was a dusty gray and the window panes were a worn white. And sitting right in the middle of the front face of the home was a large window.

The sunroom window.

I would smile and take a moment to sit and remember the times from my childhood of riding my bike, climbing the front yard tree, and throwing rocks down the driveway. I would remember the family BBQs on the back porch and my grandfather playing his Blue's records on Christmas. I would think back and laugh at remembering how uncomfortable the plastic on the living room furniture was in the summer and how steaming hot the radiators would get in the winter.

I missed my home.

I missed the memories.

And while thinking and considering these things, for a moment I felt calm. I felt okay. As I would sit and reminisce, I was temporarily whisked away to a time when there was no misery or grief. I was a child again and my invincible mother was still alive. Cooking dinner, crocheting blankets, laughing on the phone, helping me with my homework, and overall living a great life.

However, my beautiful memories didn't last long.

Just as any other moment, I would quickly snap back to reality. And immediately those precious memories were shattered as my mind would revert back to the final traumatic memories in the very same home that I loved so much.

The hospital bed…

The medications…

Seeing my mother in pain…

The sound of the endless prayers that I seemed to pray in vain… The beckoning call downstairs…

Her last breath…

With these latter thoughts, anger surged through me.

I quickly changed my mind: I hated that house. And I would never love it again. And that was the end of it.

I discontinued my random drives to my childhood home. I had to accept that there was nothing there for me anymore. The bad memories seemed to outweigh the good. I had no reason to return.

Holidays and my childhood home were now nothing more than a currently miserable experience and a sad past memory.

However, still broken in my spirit, my quest for peace didn't stop there. I began to desire the comfort of people in hopes to alleviate my pain.

Dangerously, I began to place my confidence in people in an unhealthy way. Relying on people to somehow fill a void and make me feel whole again. I sought joy in my personal relationships with people. Becoming overly clingy in friendships and family relationships. Looking to compensate for the love that I felt I had lost. Battling with extreme loneliness, I desired to be attached to someone. I formed an unrealistic expectation for someone to be close to and rely on. And when my personal expectations were unmet repeatedly by various people, (unintentionally) my mind was consumed with feelings of rejection. I questioned whether I was loved and or concerned for. My perception of my personal value and worth was thwarted.

Did I do something wrong? I would ask myself.

Unknowingly, I was using people as a crutch for my pain. I felt lost.

And although I couldn't recognize it, I was also at the beginning stages of depression.

"He hath fenced up my way that I cannot pass, and he
hath set darkness in my paths."
– Job 19:7

Undiagnosed

*Depression is defined as a mental condition that's characterized
by feelings of despondency (loss of hope) that negatively affects how
you think, feel and behave. The effects can be seen emotionally,
psychologically and physically.*

*Signs of depression include anxiety, discontent, loss of interest,
guilt, mood swings, irritability, social isolation, excessive crying,
restlessness, remaining in a cycle of melancholy thoughts.*

For approximately 4 years after my mother's death, I struggled
with depression. At times it felt as though I was literally
spiraling out of control with emotions. Although I was unable to
identify the depression initially, the signs were there.

Why mention her if she's dead and never coming back?? These
were my harsh, yet honest thoughts as family members and
friends would sit and mention memories of my mother. I would
sit stiff and silent or force a fake smile and laugh as lighthearted
memories were shared. For every mention, my heart would ache.

It's not that the memories shared weren't special or endearing,
but I was at a place emotionally where I was completely exhausted
and I wanted to escape from the grief of losing her. Even if it
required the drastic decision of no longer mentioning her. No
more stories and no more photographs! I was over it! Sitting and

reliving old memories of my mother felt like salt being poured into a fresh wound. I loved my mother, but I no longer wanted to think about her. I wanted to force myself to forget. I saw no purpose and or benefit in remembering. The thoughts of her only caused me torment. Relieving old times weren't going to bring her back. I wanted to detach and move on with my life.

But moving on wasn't that easy.

For almost a year after her death I was successful in avoiding visiting the cemetery to view her grave. I hadn't taken the time to go since the funeral services. But as the months went by I felt shameful in not going and at least acknowledging that she was buried there. I was in fact her only child and I knew it was only right to go and visit her burial site.

One morning I woke up and made a decision to finally go to the graveyard. As I was preparing to leave, I purposely left without telling my parents where I was going. I had my own personal car so I knew leaving out unaware wouldn't be hard to do. To clarify, it's not that going to the graveyard was a secret, but my intent was to avoid any sympathetic remarks before and after I went. I wasn't looking to have an emotional breakdown in front of anyone. I wanted to be completely numb, rather detached. I knew that this eventful day could consist of many tears and emotional triggers. So, I wanted to keep myself emotionally detached as much as I could.

I'm just visiting… I continued to tell myself.

Once again, I was attempting to cope with my pain.

So, I left my home as swiftly as I could and headed to the graveyard. As I approached the cemetery gate, ironically it began to rain. A gray sky and large dark clouds quickly consumed the graveyard. Not the faintest ray of sun was visible. This unexpected weather simply mirrored my emotions and the gloomy occasion:

death and sadness. I continued to drive and ease my way as I tried to recall the exact route that was taken months earlier as I rode in the funeral car behind the hearse that carried my mother. Too proud to ask my father, someone that knew exactly where she was buried, I decided I would

figure out on my own. *I don't need help.* I harshly said to myself. *I'm fine. I can find it.*

I can't recall how long I drove until I finally found her grave, but when I did, I set the gear in park and continued to sit in the car.

Minutes passed, and I continued to sit.

Now what? What am I supposed to do?

I wanted to get out, but I was hesitant. My thoughts were rapidly going, but my body was completely still. It felt like an eternity as time passed by. I had no decorations, no one else with me, and no course or set plan of action. I was just THERE.

As I continued to sit idle, it wasn't long before my tears seemed to outnumber the drops of rain that poured down against my car. Gloom and darkness consumed me just as it did the graveyard I was in.

How am I here right now?
I'm not supposed to be here!
She wasn't supposed to die!
She should still be alive!
I knew I shouldn't have come.

Without even stepping one foot out of the car, I put the car gear in shift and drove off. I questioned whether I should have made the visit. I wanted to go, but I wasn't sure if I was ready. And I had no idea of when I would be. The experience just seemed to be another painful memory added to my running list.

At seventeen years old I felt like my life had fallen apart.

What did I do to deserve this? Why would God do this to me?

Desperate to Escape

Life continued on after I visited the graveyard. From day to day, I continued to function and partake in my ordinary everyday activities as best as I could, but I soon began to cope with my pain in an unhealthy way once again. Willingly, I began to isolate myself from others and the world around me. This new behavior being the opposite of my constant need for people that I had prior. To cope, I would confine myself to my bedroom. It sounds understandable and innocent enough, but by doing so I was creating a dangerous habit. Clouded by grief, my intent was to get a breather. In other words, escaping from anyone or anything that reminded me of my loss. For in public, even months later, I was still approached by people that would give me their condolences. Every encounter was just as painful as the ones I initially received when the death originally happened. So, in response, I felt the need to avoid people as much as I could. And regarding my new home, with my father and stepmother, I didn't have to encounter people as when I did in public, but I was still greeted with photographs and keepsakes of my mother around the house. It was a loving gesture that was made by my parents to allow me to feel at home and comfortable, but unfortunately it caused more inward turmoil than peace. And although I felt this way, I didn't have the heart to tell my parents. So, I decided to remain quiet about it. The photos and keepsakes were painful reminders that she was no longer here. I would look at her beautiful face in the photograph. So youthful, healthy, and so full and in an instant my mind would have a flashback to her appearance when she passed: Small, gaunt and withered due to the cancer. Decreasing to a weight of under one hundred pounds. Her former days in comparison to her last days were two completely different appearances and conditions. My stomach would begin to tighten and ache when I thought about not only her waning appearance, but also the excruciating memories of her sickness. Embedded into my mind were the terrible memories of her vomiting uncontrollably and the medications she constantly had to take. This being a few of the many things that haunted me. Some aspects of her sickness are too painful to even mention.

If only I could erase the memories. I thought to myself. I hated the photos. I didn't want to remember.

With this being said, my bedroom became my designated place of escape as well as hiding. A majority of my time was spent secluded away in my room with the door shut by myself. Within those four walls I was able to remove myself from the eyes of others and excessively cry and mourn. Free from judgement and pity. Free from overwhelming questions. At times I would even sit in the dark and be consumed by the silence. Sometimes the quietness put me at ease. It was comforting. It allowed me to think without interruption as I tried to make sense of my new life while also reminiscing on my old one.

My room also became a place of protection. In my mind, I was protecting myself from anything that could incite or burden me with more grief. People, things, places, memories, anything.

Hiding away from people and places became manageable for the most part. But there was one person that regardless of what I did or where I went I wasn't able to escape from.

And that person was myself.

I would never admit it, but I carried personal guilt for my mother's death. Along with feeling slighted by God, I also felt as though I had failed my mother at her most critical time. Constantly I asked myself over and over if I had done enough to help her or if something else could have been done. I felt as though I allowed her life to slip right through my hands.

What if I had fasted more consistently…

Did I clean the house enough? Were there hidden bacteria that could have spurred her death?

Maybe if I had contacted more saints to pray…

I heard a plant-based diet helps fight cancer. Maybe if I bought different foods…

Some of my reasonings and thoughts were irrational, but at the time I considered them to be real possibilities.

Valid reasons or not, I continued to feel disappointed in myself. Day in and day out I contemplated different approaches I could have taken to possibly save my mother's life. The more I considered the options, the worse I felt.

The worse I felt, the more I began to loathe myself. Even seeing my own reflection in the mirror every morning became difficult.

Unlike what others saw, I didn't see the face of a young beautiful woman with extraordinary potential. Nor did I see someone who would eventually be an overcomer. But instead, I saw a failure. An utter disappointment.

It was almost as if I could see the word disappointment subtly etched into the skin of my face. As if it was touchable. Too deeply embedded to simply wash away and too dark and potent for makeup to cover.

From my view it was permanently written all over me. I could feel it and see it. And I figured others could also.

I wonder if God is disappointed in me, too?

That thought alone was almost unbearable.

So, in my room is where I continued to hide away.

In a desperate attempt to possibly relive a happier time in my life and attempt to transform my room into a place that was pleasant, I took it upon myself to paint and decorate. Being secluded away in my room allowed a lot of time for me to change the way it looked. The original painting of the walls was dark green. So, I decided to paint and decorate it just as it was in my childhood home: Light blue walls with hand painted clouds. With stars to accommodate the overall look. All of this resembling the beloved sky. With this new endeavor I was very grateful that my parents were more than willing to provide the materials needed to make this possible. So, with cans of paint, rollers, brushes and an eager mind, I spent hours into the night remaking the former room that I loved so much. Tirelessly I worked and in about two weeks' time I finally finished. Once done I felt as though I had accomplished something great. I sat back and relished at my work.

For a moment I felt restful. I enjoyed what I had created. But something changed.

Not many weeks after I had completed the task, I sadly realized that the emotional connection was no longer the same. The room was full of color and beauty, but still empty. The walls sported inspirational quotes, yet still deep down I felt discouraged.

The appearance of the room was the same… but I wasn't the same.

Even the sun rays that shined through the windows made little to no difference.

Death and grief had changed everything. Once again, in an attempt to find joy, death had won.

It would take more than paint and decor to compensate for the loss I had suffered. It was at this moment that I fully understood that tangible things can't bring healing. But even with this knowledge I continued to seclude myself in my room. I honestly didn't know what else to do. So, I continued to do what was familiar.

It wasn't long before my loved ones began to notice my constant isolation.

Like any concerned parent, my father took the time to openly talk and discuss the issue with me. Being greatly concerned about me and also taking into consideration the loss I had suffered, he understood and wanted to reach out to me in love. But being naïve, I considered it to be a small issue. In my mind my habit wasn't unhealthy or detrimental at all, but in fact helpful. In my mind, I simply needed time alone.

Sadly, grief had blinded me to what others could clearly see. I was in a dangerous place and I couldn't see it. My choice to constantly remain secluded was only heightening my depression.

My isolation and withdrawal from others didn't simply stop within the four walls of my rooms, but also it encompassed extracurricular activities at school. From my freshman to my junior year in high school I participated in sports and clubs. Basketball, track & field, cross country, yearbook club to name a few. But during this time after my mother's passing, I chose not to be involved. I was grateful for the friends I made and although I was encouraged by others to continue participating, I knew it was best not to. I had lost all passion for the activities. Things were different now. My focus had changed. Instead, with college in my near future, I decided to channel my energy into my academics. I had always excelled in school, but I wanted to be certain my honor status remained intact. Engrossing myself in my school work also helped to preoccupy my mind from my pain. Overall, I worked and pushed my way through my senior year and graduated in May 2010.

*"Thou tellest my wanderings: put thou my tears into thy
bottle: [are they] not in thy book?"*
– Psalm 56:8

Desperate to Breath

In August 2010 I continued my education as a college freshman at Parkland CC in Champaign-Urbana. I was finally beginning a new chapter in my life and I was excited for it.

The city of Champaign Urbana is located only thirty minutes away from my hometown of Danville. With my choice to move, many questioned why I chose to attend a community college in another city when I had the same opportunity right in town. (Danville)

For reasons that only a griever would fully understand I chose not to explain. But in response I simply let them know that it was a personal choice of mine. As an explanation for my personal choice, I still struggled with depression and intentionally remaining isolated from others. With this move, I wanted to be away from the town I had always known. Escaping from the town itself and the memories it held. In no way did I regret the life I had in Danville, but I wanted to temporarily disconnect from it. Still in my mind, I needed room to breathe. Living in a different city in a new environment allowed me to have a *breather* from what felt like constant suffocation.

In a new city I no longer had to find ways to avoid the cemetery. In a new city I no longer had to encounter sympathetic looks from those that felt sorry for me.

In a new city I no longer had to avoid my childhood home.

By moving, I was temporarily free from it all. I had found an escape, and I willingly took it. I was more than desperate to find a way to cope with the loss I had just suffered only a year prior and moving was my choice of action.

With this new transition I was not only embarking on receiving my degree, but just as much I was now entering into adulthood being now eighteen years old. For the last two years my life had been an unexpected whirlwind of change. Ages sixteen, seventeen, and eighteen were anything but spectacular. I went from being an ordinary teenager to being a caretaker of a cancer patient and now a griever. And in addition, a new full time college student. Life had definitely taken me for a spin.

With all this being said, I had to sit down and reflect on my life. Asking myself *Who am I now?*

Who am I supposed to be?

With the life changing events that had taken place in two years I realized I wasn't the same person anymore. My perspective and psyche had changed. I saw life and the world differently now.

I began to question my identity and my purpose. The unpredictability of life had taken a toll on me.

However, even with so much on my mind, school kept me preoccupied. During the week I attended classes and studied constantly. Then, on the weekends I was dedicated to work, family, friends and attending service at my local church.

God's House.

At times it was extremely difficult to go, but I still continued to attend. Although my mother had been gone for over a year, my discontent and heartbreak towards God remained the same.

God I just don't understand…

My Sunday mornings had lost its zeal. My eagerness to get to God's House had changed. The eagerness I once had was now stifled by my pain, grief and bitterness.

Simply, I couldn't understand God's decision. And although I was bitter regarding my circumstances, I continued to display a facade when entering into the church house and fellowshipping with the other believers. Outwardly I wanted to appear as though my relationship with God was just as strong as it had ever been. Unwilling to appear weak and fragile or in need of help.

In my mind, I think I actually believed I had God deceived too. As I had always done, I continued to operate in my roles and positions, but deep down I was angry and offended by God.

As the service would begin and go forward, the presence of God would undoubtedly enter the building. Moving people out of their seats to the altar and propelling the minister to begin profoundly speaking on the Word of God as the Spirit and anointing of God overwhelmed them. Yet, in the midst of such an amazing experience, there were times that I would rigidly praise God or make a rash decision to leave the service early. I was allowing my flesh to pivot me to withhold worship from God. It's as if I could literally feel my flesh and the Spirit grappling with one another as each tried to take claim of my mind, body and emotions.

And just like the feelings that came initially at the time of my mother's death, I didn't know how to process any of the thoughts and emotions that were overwhelming me a year later. I felt lost. And of a surety I was miserable.

I just wanted my normal life back.

As I would exit the church after service and make my way to my car I would silently ask within myself *God, what did I do to deserve this?*

A question that seemed unanswerable.

Eclipsed

Should I even answer?
My stomach began to churn as once again my phone unexpectedly began to ring from an incoming call.

Lord, please not someone else…

Within the short three to four years after my mother's passing, I was repeatedly revisited by death and grief.

Some expectedly, others not. Sadly, enough some of the deaths were within a few weeks of each other. It was absolutely mind blowing. It had gotten to a point that when my phone would ring at random times in the night or in the early morning or while in class on campus, I would immediately begin to panic. Uncertain as to what the caller may have to say. Receiving news that a loved one had been admitted into the hospital or that *they weren't doing too well,* I automatically assumed that death was near.

The conversation was almost always the same.

Keep them in your prayers… the caller would say.

Hearing that request temporarily paralyzed me. It was difficult to hear.

Upon hearing this, in my mind I would reflect back to the nights that I would cry out to God in prayer. Sobbing and weeping as I requested healing for my mother.

Keep them in your prayers…

It was like a resounding echo in my hollow and broken heart.

To name by relation, I lost a grandfather, three aunts, a cousin, and three members from my church congregation. Death had become like a vicious cycle that wouldn't stop. In culmination I attended approximately twelve funerals during this time.

With so many more deaths that had occurred I felt as though my progress towards healing was being hindered. It felt as though there was no time to recuperate from one death to the next.

Once again, I found myself overwhelmed with anxiety paranoia.

Will my father be next?

My stepmother?

Best friend? ME?

With this being said, sadly the news of death became the norm, while receiving news of good health and restoration became unexpected and abnormal.

The last phone conversations, hospital visits, holidays, birthday celebrations, family gatherings, all flashed in my mind when hearing that another loved one had left this earth. And when it came time to say goodbye, I once again had to muster up the strength to walk down a dreary church aisle and stand before a steel coffin that simply held the empty corpse of someone I once knew.

The last four years of my life had consisted of constant *goodbyes*.

And like a time warp, I would flashback to the first funeral I ever attended at five years old. I would compare my experience then to what I was currently experiencing. Reflecting on how innocent and naïve I was as a young child regarding the concept of death. It was foreign, and I was completely detached from it. There was no familiarity or emotional connection to it at all. I hadn't experienced it, nor did I understand it. But by my late teens and early twenties my stance was the complete opposite.

I longed to be that naïve five-year-old again. I was restless and beyond tired.

Am I ever going to have peace? I began to ask myself this question. Peace.

I longed for it.

Just rehearsing the word in my thoughts caused a scripture to surface in my mind.

"Thou wilt keep him in perfect peace, whose mind is stayed on thee," Isaiah 26:3.

It was one of my grandmother's beloved scriptures. I had heard the scripture since I was a child and I was more than familiar with it. She too had passed away by this time in my life, but still her teachings remained deep down inside of me. And as I sat and reflected on my life for the last two years I had to ask myself the question,

What is true peace?

As I thought about it, I had to be honest, I didn't have an answer. At one point I thought I did know.

I quietly collected myself and sat for a moment. Laying at the end of my bed was my Bible. I grabbed a hold of it and kneeled down on the side of my bed and began to read the scripture in Isaiah.

I quickly stopped.

As I began to read, it felt as though a dart had been thrown directly into my heart.

Turning my eyes in the other direction I closed the burgundy leather cover and pushed the Bible aside.

I was torn.

I'm setting myself up for disappointment again, I sadly thought.

I wanted peace, and I desperately needed peace, but I didn't know if it was a possibility for me. In my mind, attempting to seek peace could prove to be as futile as my attempt for seeking healing from God. I questioned if this time would be any different and if my prayer would be answered or even heard.

Since the death of my mother, I had gotten to a place in my life where I began to question my faith. The same faith that I proclaimed and held dear even prior to learning about my mother's illness. And most certainly after she was diagnosed.

But I had gotten to a place that spiritually I had never been before. Pondering and asking questions that seemed unanswerable. And having doubts and feelings I never fathomed that I would.

Like a lost child, over and over I asked myself *Where am I?*

Faith wise, it was as if I was aimlessly wandering.

Staggering as I struggled to keep my balance while

teeter-tottering on what felt like the edge of the universe. Having no certainty as to whether or not I had the strength to keep my footing or if I'd completely spiral downward into a merciless abyss.

Being one missed step away from cascading into a place that was deep and far gone from the very thing that once kept me grounded.

Where am I?

Where's my faith?

Where's the light?

My radiant faith had become overshadowed and dimmed. Just as a solar eclipse, my faith was being overpowered by a mass that was pervasive and dark.

This being death and grief.

Thus, causing my world to feel dark and cold.

I felt as though death had stripped me of ever having the opportunity to have real peace again.

I wanted to have peace again.
But could I?
Should I even hope for it?
The scripture continued to play in my mind...
"Thou wilt keep him in perfect peace, whose mind is stayed on thee: because he trusteth in thee," Isaiah 26:3

Facing the Dark

Do I really need this? …
I can manage this by myself. I just need time.
I think I'm alright. …
Aren't I?
No. I am NOT alright. And I haven't been in a long time.
I need to go. …

As I got myself dressed and grabbed my car keys to attend my first counseling/wellness appointment I was bombarded with conflicting thoughts as to whether or not I needed to see a specialist. The year was 2012, and it had been three years since my mother had passed. My pride and stubbornness were telling me that I was okay and that I could manage it with time and patience. But deep down I knew this wasn't true. And those that were close to me knew it wasn't either. So, in love, it was suggested by a reputable friend that I take a new direction. This being seeking and accepting specialized help.

Initially, I felt slighted that counseling was even suggested. But I came to a place where I realized that my mental health was suffering and greatly at stake. It was as if I was trapped in an emotional and mental whirlwind that I couldn't get out of. I had moments where I felt uplifted as if the grief had finally subsided, but then there were days that I felt completely consumed by it as if it were taking over my life.

It was a relentless cycle.

And to add to my troubles, I had sadly even gotten to a place where I began to contemplate suicide.

I had to be honest with myself and realize that I desperately needed help. My grief had now become a life or death situation.

I will never forget my first session. It was a Tuesday near the time of sundown. I arrived at the office anxious and nervous as to what would take place that day. I remember sitting in my car thinking to myself *Okay, I'll only tell a little of my story.. Not too much. Keep it basic.* When I got out of my car and entered the building, the walk up to the office was nerve racking. The halls were quiet and empty and the stairs leading to the upstairs offices seemed endless.

I questioned if I had the right decision in coming. But having come this far, I didn't want to leave and return home.

After searching for a short time, I found the office where my sessions would take place.

In contrast to how I originally felt, when I entered the office my nerves were calmed a bit. I was welcomed in and warmly greeted by the counselor. I was directed to a set of chairs to sit and make myself comfortable at. Obliging, I took a seat and sat almost completely stiff. I was uncertain as to what would happen next. I'm sure my facial expression told it all.

As the session began and the counselor began to talk, I began to feel better about choosing to come. I could tell by the demeanor and approach of the counselor that they were not only gifted and experienced, but that there was in fact a genuine concern about my wellbeing. I began to feel confident in opening up and telling my story. I was honestly taken aback. The more I spoke, the easier it became to continue speaking. From the counselor, direct eye contact was given, scriptures were used, wisdom was provided and no interruptions or assumptions were made as I told my story. There was no awkward reaction as I began to sob and there was no misunderstanding as I shared my personal thoughts and feelings. I was assured that what I felt and was experiencing was normal and that overcoming it all was more than possible.

What I intended to be a one hour session turned into about three. Thankfully time wasn't a concern on behalf of the counselor. So, as I sat and poured out, allowing myself to be broken, I completely abandoned my original plan of keeping it *basic*. Without question I had cried many days and nights within the last few years, but the tears shed on the day of my first session outnumbered them all. Words can't describe the euphoric feeling I felt as I was able to calmly sit and be vulnerable by expressing the woes I had carried for so long. The counseling I received was spiritually based and of a surety the Spirit of God was there in the office along with us.

I could feel weights breaking from off of my mind and my heart as I sat and relived my life for the past four years:

My mother's diagnosis.. Having faith for healing.. Her death…

The confusion..

The anger towards God.. Family issues..

The sleepless nights… Leaving my hometown… Losing multiple loved ones.. Wanting to end it all..

Everything.

By the time the session was finished, nightfall had come. And as things were coming to a close, I knew I had made the right choice in coming.

As I left that evening from my session I was glad that I was able to overcome my initial uneasiness in receiving help. That night I learned that receiving help isn't a sign of weakness, but rather a sign of courage and strength.

When I arrived back at my apartment that evening I took a moment to go and see my reflection in the bathroom mirror. It was an extremely emotional night, and I was sure my face told it all. When looking in the mirror, looking back at me were red swollen eyes and a face that was puffy and tear-stained. Dark circles complementing it all. I was absolutely fatigued, and I looked absolutely terrible. But unlike how I looked, I felt amazing. And as I continued to look at my reflection, even the subtle etchings of *disappointment* that once plagued my reflection were beginning to fade.

Already, I was beginning to heal.

After my first initial counseling session I had an appointment every week for the next few months. As I progressed, my sessions were set for every few weeks and then every few months. More tears were shed and more wounds were revealed, but with diligence I was enlightened and properly instructed on how to address the grief and the burdens that came with it. These new ideas and approaches were foreign to me, but with one on one teaching from my counselor I began to understand. With time I was made aware of how to healthfully address the negative effects and triggers that pain and grief can create within the psyche. I had to learn to become self-aware and conscious of my behaviors and thoughts. Understanding that my mind was vulnerable due to the significant loss and that it would take self-determination and well thought out healing strategies to renew and stabilize it. Furthermore, and most importantly, I learned how to strengthen my relationship with the Lord. Understanding that my spiritual life was the core and catalyst to becoming fully healed.

Choosing to adhere to wisdom and receive counseling was one the best decisions I ever made for my overall wellbeing.

There was so much knowledge and wisdom I obtained from my sessions that it is impossible to mention and fully explain it all. However, there are significant scriptures, notes, truths, and affirmations that I want to mention:

- Romans 12:1

- I Peter 5:7

- Isaiah 55: 8-11

- St. John 11:25-26

- II Corinthians 10:3-5

- Philippians 4:4-8

1. We must accept the death of the loved one. Understanding that although it is painful, we have to trust God's decision and sovereignty.

2. Remember and celebrate the years, days and moments you had with your loved one.

3. It's okay to remember. We don't have to force ourselves to forget.

4. Speak openly to God about exactly how you feel. Whether it's confusion, anger, sadness, loneliness or fear. He already knows, but He wants us to be vulnerable and honest with Him. Vulnerability with God leads to deliverance. Pride will keep us hostage.

5. Every single day we have to make a conscious effort to fight against negative thoughts and replace them with positive healthy ones.

6. Acknowledge and reveal every emotion, feeling, pain or question you may have had toward your deceased loved one. Verbally speak it aloud so that it can be exposed and healed. No longer causing you turmoil and unrest on the inside.

7. You have power over your emotions. Grieving is natural and necessary, but make a conscious decision to not allow your emotions to influence you to do anything that is unhealthy and harmful to yourself and or others.

8. Ask God to help you forgive those that have wounded you. Understand that it really isn't personal. They have their own unresolved pains and personal issues. Wounded people wound others.

9. People or things will never be able to fill the void that we feel, only God can. Without Him we'll always feel broken and empty.

10. Understand that no experience or time of suffering is wasted. God is going to use you to help bring deliverance to someone else. He heals us as we help heal others.

11. Pay attention to any emotional triggers you may have. Don't overlook any unhealthy behaviors. It all must be addressed.

12. Satan preys on us when we're emotionally vulnerable. We have to stay consistently connected to God so we won't be led astray.

13. Your life doesn't end because you've experienced death. Your life still has great purpose even after death has ravaged through your life.

Opened Eyes

Small, yet progressive steps were being made in my healing and personal walk with God. To say that I was all inclusively restored immediately after first receiving specialized help wouldn't be factual. There were times that my progress was excellent and there were also times that I failed miserably. It was a tedious process. However, with the knowledge I had acquired and support that I had, I was on my way to coming out of the dark place I was in.

I was very grateful for the help that I was receiving and the life changing effect that it had. Leading me down the path to come to terms and reevaluate my relationship with God and my mindset. With this needed help, I was learning how to properly process and accept death, but even more so I was learning how to focus on obtaining and living a joyful spirit filled life despite death.

Having my mind enlightened, I was able to soberly assess my life and the challenges that I faced. Viewing things from a perspective of hope and no longer one of despair.

With this enlightenment, I came to a place where I desired to trust and fully embrace God again. No longer resenting Him and being bitter, but instead desiring and longing to be close to Him.

I now had a change of heart.

Beforehand, when I was blinded by grief, I could only see the pain and agony that accompanied the loss of my mother. Allowing myself to be consumed in anger and bitterness, I was completely negligent of how faithful and graceful God had been to me throughout it all.

I was so focused on death that I overlooked the gift of life that had been granted to me.

Healing had opened my eyes. I could see clearly now.

I began to reflect on how gracious God had been to me. Like a checklist, I began to count each moment and divine encounter that I had during my most challenging time.

To begin, I began to thank the Lord for giving me the opportunity to have a relationship with my mother. Not merely just being birthed by her, but even more so being able to build and have precious memories with her. Being able to experience the love and tenderness of a good mother as well as receiving the discipline and wisdom of one too. I was grateful that, although I was a teenager when she passed away, my mother was present for every significant milestone in my life. And I knew that if she were still alive, she'd still be by my side as an active presence just as she was before. Advising and guiding me on how to become a well-rounded, sound minded, educated, caring, and self-driven woman that lived up to her highest potential. Just as she was herself.

Not even something as permanent as death could take away the memories I shared with her and the life lessons she taught me. I was grateful for the time that God graced us to have.

With this, I also began to praise and thank God for guarding my heart and mind during this critical time. For although I was overwhelmed with the many tumultuous emotions that come with grief, I never reached a place where I fully succumbed to the mental breakdown that was beginning to take place in my mind. For with His mighty hand, the Lord quickly grabbed and caught a hold of me before I fell over the edge. Stabilizing me and providing me the mental strength to hold fast to my life without doing anything that was negatively radical or extreme. The Lord gave me a reason to continue living.

Even in my pain, the blessings of God were present in my life. And one by one I began to acknowledge each blessing. Acknowledging the painful moments, but giving God glory for the blessings that overshadowed it.

Yes, I missed my childhood home with my mother, but I had a place to call home with my father and stepmother.

Yes, I suffered with feelings of loneliness, but still I had a special circle of family and friends that loved and supported me.

Yes, at times it was hard to focus on my academics, but still I graduated from High School with honors. Thereafter enrolling into college and successfully continuing my education.

Yes, at times I felt weak physically. But still I was in fact strong and healthy. My health didn't deteriorate with the grief.

Yes, I almost reached my breaking point, but just in time I was able to receive direct access to specialized help.

I was healing.
I was ALIVE.
And most of all, God loved me.

And it was His relentless love that kept and covered me through it all. Through every moment of pain, disappointment, anger, bitterness, confusion, loneliness, fear, and attack, He never left my side.

He was with me the entire time.

And although I couldn't see it, God's love and protection had been a halo of light that fully hovered over and around me during the darkest time of my life.

The power of darkness had proved itself futile against the God of light. And this alone was a reason to rejoice.

Tears began to fall as I considered and counted all the blessings of God. I began to sob greatly. But this time not because of death, but instead because of **life**. I knew that from this point forward my life would never be the same. I made a decision that I would no longer sit hopelessly in the dark as the terrors of night overwhelmed me, but instead I would position myself to see the sun rise again. Anticipating the greatest morning I would ever experience.

"I need to have a fresh start," I spoke aloud to myself, and that's exactly what I set my mind to do.

A Divine Opportunity

Repentance. Acknowledging that we have caused an offense to God and being willing to take full accountability for it. Repentance requires making a conscious decision to discontinue in the offensive act so that the severed relationship between ourselves and God can be redeemed.

Upon hearing and seeing the word repentance, many of us experience feelings of condemnation. Feeling condemned and ashamed for the natural and spiritual detrimental choices we've personally made. This is one aspect of repentance.

However, repentance should also be viewed as an awesome life changing opportunity. A divine opportunity that humbly positions us to become free from any behaviors, choices, mindsets and lifestyles that have brought ruin to our natural and spiritual lives. In contrast to what many may personally think about the concept of repentance, it should in fact stir up feelings of joy and not disheartenment. Repentance is a beautiful gift from God that allows us to become and remain close to Him. It is the catalyst for a changed heart and allows us to be rescued from the peril of non-repentance. (II Corinthians 7:10)

Being close to God and remaining so, is what I desperately wanted and needed in my life. I never wanted to experience a time in my life again where I felt distant from Him. I wanted a fresh and new start in my relationship with the Lord. I had had one since I was a child, but I now wanted one that was better and stronger than the one before.

And in order to obtain a greater relationship than what I currently had, repentance was required. I needed to repent from the offensive and carnal mindset that I had towards God when grieving. The ugliness of my pride was evident: I questioned and accused Him of being unfair and insensitive. And while continuing in my spiritual journey, I refused to be fully surrendered to Him. Being only willing to give Him a fraction, or part of me. And in an idolatrous way I placed my personal desire over His perfect Will. Yes, praying for mother to be healed was noble, but becoming grudgeful against the Lord once she passed was not. For one of the most important aspects of living for God is accepting and reverencing the Lord's sovereignty. Understanding that every decision that the Lord makes and every experience that He allows is all a part of His perfect plan for our lives. Whether these experiences are joy filled or sorrowful, they each have a divine purpose.

With a contrite spirit and an open heart, I began to freely pray and repent to God. Asking for forgiveness and also humbly asking for help. Relaying to Him my desire for a fresh start and a revived relationship with Him.

But this time in a different way.

I no longer desired to be stale and bitter, but instead I wanted to be completely refreshed. I wanted every aspect of my relationship with God to mature and be heightened. My approach to prayer and fasting, my appearance, my involvement in ministries, my interactions with people, and most of all my mind and heart. I desired a change in every area of my life.

It was my heartfelt desire to rekindle a fiery zeal for God and I was more than willing to change, implement, and sacrifice whatever was needed in order to make it happen.

As time progressed and I made my new mind and life changes, my relationship with God had become renewed. God had literally become my everything. The very heart in my chest pulsed for Him. But this alone didn't satisfy my appetite. I wanted even more. In addition to my renewed fiery zeal, I also wanted to forge another aspect of our relationship:

A friendship.

I wanted to become friends with God.

Initially, the idea of becoming friends with God seemed odd and foreign. I chuckled to myself even when considering it. I thought to myself *How do you become friends with God? I mean, you can't even see Him!*

I had never realized it before, but for so long I narrow mindedly viewed God simply in the role of a Ruler, Protector, Provider, Father and an awe striking Wonder. In addition, I viewed Him as an All Knowing being that was to be revered for His power and incomparable acts.

These roles are in fact true to God's character and worthy of praise, however His greatness goes beyond these roles.

With a matured spiritual understanding, I realized that He wasn't just some Mighty Ruler that sat in the heavens producing powerful works like a machine, but instead He was also a loving friend. A friend that regardless of how great of a position and how many roles He fulfilled, He always made Himself available to those that needed Him. Being sensitive to our needs and constantly reaching out in love. Even when we're unwilling to receive it. And like a faithful friend, He was there to stand by our side through every high and low season of our life.

Proving Himself to be an extremely personal and understanding God and not a distant lofty one. Without question, God was the greatest friend anyone could ever have. And the bond I began to form with Him was unlike anything I had ever experienced before.

Like a friend in the natural realm, I began spending quality time with God. For just like an earthly friendship, the only way that a relationship can become strong and continue to be so is if there is plenty of bonding time. So, outside of prayer, I would sit and casually talk to God just as I would a friend. Making sure to speak to the Lord as if He was literally in the room with me. Taking into account that although He is an invisible God, I could make myself comfortable and free enough to enjoy His presence although my natural eye couldn't see Him. With this new endeavor, I would intentionally set aside time every day to openly discuss any and all matters to and with Him. Being vulnerable, yet secure enough to freely relay my concerns, fears, aspirations, joys, failures and all other heartfelt matters. Knowing that He is always an ear to listen and a voice of encouragement and wisdom.

The Lord literally became my best friend. It was during this time that I also took the initiative to also tell the Lord my heartfelt feelings regarding my mother passing away. Not in a grudgeful way, but simply opening up about the pain I felt and the difficulties I faced from it. I wanted to be honest with Him. For I understood that God wouldn't love me any less if I spoke to Him about how I felt rejected and abandoned by Him when I lost my mother. I knew He would understand and receive my honesty and love me through the pain.

And from this moment I learned one of the greatest lessons of my life: Honesty leads to healing. Our healing is completely dependent on how honest we are about our condition. Our mental, emotional and spiritual wellbeing is dependent upon it. For it is through the uncomfortable, yet necessary pains of honesty that healing is birthed. It is impossible to be healed if we're unwilling to address and openly speak about the issues that are the source of our wounds.

I was grateful for this revelation that the Lord had given me.

And as time went on, I continued to freely open myself up to God. And in turn, it's as if God began to open Himself up to me. I began to discover and learn things about God and His character that I never knew before. This new knowledge coming from Him as He directly spoke through His voice, in dreams, preached sermons, and personally studying His Word/scriptures. This experience was remarkable. It's as if I was meeting Him again for the first time. I had never known God in this way before.

The horizon looked bright.

"For thou art my lamp, O LORD: and the LORD
will lighten my darkness."
– II Samuel 22:29

Sun Kissed

There she is! Congratulations! She is beautiful!
My heart swelled up with joy as the nurse delicately handed me my newborn daughter. She was full faced with a head full of hair.

Weighing eight pounds four ounces. To me, she was absolutely perfect, and I loved her with all my heart.

To the left side of the hospital bed was my husband, Arron. Full of joy I glanced over at him to see his reaction to our newborn daughter.

When looking at him it was amazing to see the endearment in his eyes as he looked at our first child. I knew he loved her just as much as I did and would do everything possible to cherish and protect her. I could see it in his eyes. I knew he would be a great father.

Months prior to the birth, my husband and I chose our daughter's name. And with no hesitation we decided to name her Vanessa.

It seemed befitting to name her after my mother. And I was glad to do so.

Vanessa M. Lipscomb.

As first time parents, this experience was very exciting, but also nerve-racking as first time parents. But thankfully we had a great support team to help us. This being our natural parents and also other extended love ones that were physically there with us during this beautiful life changing moment. Standing on the other side of the room was our good friend and also Vanessa's godmother, Ericka. And also with us was Cathy. Just as she had been present for the passing of my mother, she was also now here for the birth of our daughter. Even with so much going on, I couldn't help but to wonder how Cathy may have felt. Of a surety she was excited for us, but I wondered if this experience caused her to miss her son Keynon. I wondered if it triggered any emotions.

By this time, nineteen years had passed since his death. And after so many years had passed by, I wondered if it ever got to a point where it no longer hurt to miss a loved one that had passed away.

I couldn't answer that question myself.

By this time, the year 2016, my mother had been gone for seven years. I had accepted her death, but still I missed her greatly. Milestones such as this, becoming a mother myself, triggered many emotions. Causing me to miss and think of her a lot. But overall, I knew that if she were alive she'd be proud and ecstatic to be a new grandmother. Just as she had done well in raising me, I vowed to do the same with my daughter and the children to come. Her life lessons and the great example she showed permanently remained with me. Remembering her brought me great comfort. I was now at a place where I understood that it is okay to remember.

There's healing in remembering.

A Deep Sleep

I turned the worn golden door knob and stepped inside. I was in my childhood home again.

I took only a few steps inside before I stopped and stood motionless in the front entrance way. As I looked around I was unsure of what was happening or, better yet, what had happened.

Where is everything? I thought to myself.

As I continued to walk through the entrance way and into the living room, I realized that not only was the front hall empty, but the rest of the house was too. Being empty of not just furniture and decor, but even the color, paint and paneling on the walls were gone. The house had been completely stripped.

Confused, but still curious, I continued to walk through each room. It was eerie enough to see my beloved home completely bare, but in addition the house was completely silent. Nothing could be heard inside or outside of the house. Not even a creak in the floor.

What is going on?? I thought to myself.

I started to become anxious and panic as I began to scurry in and out of the rooms.

There has to be something here. Anything! I was overwhelmed and frantic as I tried to make sense of it all.

And then I woke up.

It was a dream.

It had been years since I had had dreams or nightmares about my mother and or our home. About eight years had lapsed since the last one had occurred.

Why now? I wondered.

I wasn't sure if what I had just dreamed could be identified as a dream or a nightmare, but it definitely left a deep impression on me. One that I couldn't shake. Ultimately causing me to feel unsettled. I prayed about my dream and decided to contact my Pastor about what I had experienced. I knew the dream most likely had a spiritual message/implication, but I wasn't exactly sure what it could be. From reading scripture, like in the stories of Joseph and Daniel (Genesis 37:5-11, Daniel 2:36-45), I knew it was more than likely that God wanted to reveal something important to me. But what?

I contacted my Pastor and retold the dream to him. He said that he would pray and seek God for an answer and that when he received an answer he'd contact me about it. I remained prayerful, but was nervous to say the least. Seeing that at one point in my life I was a victim to nightmares that were directly connected to my mother's passing, I wasn't at all thrilled to have experienced this dream. I had made great progress in returning to a normal sleep pattern and having peace when it was time to rest. I hated to think I might revert back to that awful period of my life.

I asked God to cover my mind and spirit while I slept. Covering it in His peace so that I could fully rest at night.

Thankfully the Lord answered my prayers for peace and rest. I didn't begin to have nightmares again, nor any more unsettling dreams.

About three weeks went by and I was contacted by my Pastor. My Pastor, Melvin Campbell Sr., relayed to me what the Lord had revealed to him through prayer. To summarize, the dream was an indicator that I currently was and had been carrying a void since the passing of my mother. This being an intensely felt absence of someone or something.

In my dream, the childhood home signified the life and the memories that I once had. A time in my life that I still desperately longed for. And when entering into the home it was made immediately evident that I was looking for someone or something to give me relief and comfort. I was overly confident that I would either see, touch, or hear something that would allow me to relive those precious times and moments.

The empty home was a dual representation: First, it indicated that although I loved that precious time of my life, being able to return to it was no longer an option. It was something I had to humbly accept although it would be difficult. And second, the home represented that I **myself** was internally void. Just as the home had empty space that was available to be filled, I did too. I carried an emptiness. The home was a mirror reflection of myself. And regardless of how much I searched, there was no item, person, or sound in life that would be able to fill that empty space within me. For only God could.

My Pastor let me know that the bond with my mother was precious and that she couldn't be replaced by anyone or anything. And that I needed to let God touch and fill the void that I had that she once filled. He told me to pray to God and ask Him to fill me with His love and peace so I could no longer be naturally and spiritually hindered by the emptiness I carried.

After receiving the interpretation of my dream, I was taken aback. It's not that I didn't believe the interpretation, but I was shocked to know that after eight years since my mother's death, I still carried a void that she once filled. My mind was blown. *But I feel fine. I've accepted her death and I've grown so much over the years. But yet I'm carrying a void??* I thought to myself. For a moment I felt as though I was seventeen again: lost and looking for answers. However, with spiritual maturity, I had to remember that God would never lead me astray, nor lie to me. The dream had purpose and carried an important message and I needed to seek Him for guidance about it. Although I was taken aback, I knew from personal experience that placing my confidence in my own opinion and feelings was an unwise thing to do. I had to trust that God had revealed all of these things to open my eyes and draw me closer to Him. Obviously, there were still areas in my mind and heart that needed to be healed. I wasn't exactly sure what, but I trusted that He would show me in due time.

Outside of the startling dream I felt okay overall. So much had changed in eight years. However, even with this being said, it wasn't long before the interpretation and the truth of the dream began to manifest itself in my life.

Unsolved Mystery

Mother's Day week 2018 was an unforgettable one. I can't recall the exact day of the week, but without question I was emotionally unsettled for the span of a few days. Completely oblivious and forgetful of the message and interpretation of the dream that was given just a few months before, I couldn't grasp why I was so emotionally tense. Everything was frustrating and my patience was short! Although I knew that Mother's Day was coming up on Sunday, I completely disregarded the idea that what I felt was in any connection to missing my mother due to the holiday. For this would have been my ninth Mother's Day without her. Years prior I loathed this holiday, but after four or five years had passed, it no longer caused me to feel distraught. I would of course think of her, but I would continue on with my day just as I did any other holiday. Making sure to contact my stepmother and grandmother to celebrate their special day. And if I decided to travel to my home town of Danville for the holiday, I would make sure to go and visit my mother's grave and decorate it. In other words, I felt strong and encouraged on Mother's Day. I was emotionally okay.

At least I thought.

I'm uncertain as to what event caused the argument or what was done, but my husband and I got into a huge dispute during this particular week of Mother's Day. The argument took place as I was leaving our home and heading to work. While driving to my job I was bubbling with what felt like a thousand different emotions. It felt as though a storm was brewing inside of me. Rapidly spinning around trying to erupt out of me. But I refused to let it. I had to muster up all the strength I could and continue on with my day.

Once I arrived at my job, I gathered myself as best as I could and made up my mind to have a normal work day. When I entered the classroom I was greeted by a small crowd of happy toddler faces that were excited to see me. It was story time, and they were eager for me to grab one of their favorite books from the shelf and begin reading to them. This too was one of my favorite times of the day. As I made my way to take a seat and begin story time with my children, suddenly an unexpected shift happened. Not in the physical classroom itself, but inside of me. And I was completely caught off guard when it happened. Although I had made an attempt to suppress it, the storm that had been brewing in my heart and spirit finally took over. I completely broke down in tears. Embarrassed and sobbing, I fled out of my classroom as my co-workers stepped in to take my place.

Unsure of where to go, I fled into the bathroom to hide. And once I was certain the door was locked, I allowed myself to continue having my emotional breakdown. It was almost like deja vu: purposely locking myself away in a room so I could excessively cry and express every emotion.

My thoughts were simple: *Mama, I miss you... Lord, help... Lord, please help...*

Completely overwhelmed with what just took place, I tried my best to piece together what had just happened. Everything had happened so fast. And to make matters worse, none of it made any sense.

What is going on?

I was no longer angry at God for my mother passing for I understood that it was His Will. This being something I had accepted some time ago.

So where did this emotional eruption come from?

I couldn't pinpoint it, but based on this episode alone, I knew I was definitely off-balanced in my heart and mind.

While staring at the bathroom walls, I realized I didn't have time while at my job to figure it all out. So, I decided to resume solving the mystery later.

Sun Spot

When I reflected on this moment later on, after leaving work and going home, I remembered the dream and the significance of it.

I could see now that I was in fact carrying a void for my mother. It was now more than evident.

By definition, the word void means a lack or emptiness. The state of being without.

And by definition and just like in the dream, I desperately longed to see, touch, hear and overall be in the presence of my mother again. The deep pain that I carried was from her absence. By 2018 so many amazing and celebratory events had taken place in my life: I had graduated from both High school and college, I had gotten married, became a mother myself and also had begun my career. The Lord had allowed me to do well and accomplish a lot over the course of nine years. However, deep down inside, even with reaching so many beautiful milestones, it felt as though I was always missing a critical piece. And I realized now that that piece was my mother.

All the celebratory moments that had taken place in my life only intensified her absence.

Without fully realizing it, during these life changing moments it was as if I was subconsciously waiting and expecting her to show up and be there just as she always had been. She was always present for every important milestone in my life.

And years later a part of me was still expecting a phone call or for a card to be sitting on the kitchen table for me with her signature on the front. Absentmindedly I would sit, fantasize and imagine in my mind what most likely would have been her reaction to the wonderful things that were taking place in my life. What she would say, her facial expression, the advice she probably would have given etc. Basically, everything I could remember about her. In truth, these fantasies I conjured up in my mind were being used as a comfort to the pain of knowing that I would never actually know.

The void I had was not only deep, but it was also full of questions and wonder.

I could see now that my startling dream was simply a direct reflection of thoughts and feelings that I had unknowingly suppressed for some time. I was oblivious to the severity of the void that I carried. But thankfully God saw fit to reveal these things to me and open my eyes through and in a dream. It was the perfect way to catch my attention. For while asleep, my mind wasn't distracted with the cares of my day to day activities. Also, while asleep I didn't have the capabilities to ignore the revelation the same way voluntarily or involuntarily I would as if I were to be conscious and awake.

Overall, all of this once again showed me God's extreme love and concern for me. He intentionally was doing everything possible to heal my wounds and restore me.

To be clear, my life was great, and I had no reason to complain about anything. God had opened many doors and had given me the strength to overcome much in nine years. However, although I was at a place in my life where everything around me gleamed bright, the void and absence of my mother was like a sun spot in my sun:

A seemingly small, yet in actuality, a large dark area that could be seen in the midst of the glow around it.

Small in comparison, but still present.

I had come far in my healing, but with all that had taken place and had been revealed, I still needed to be made whole. The definition of **whole** meaning to have no lack or areas of instability.

Being naïve and unaware of the void, I assumed that since I had come to terms and accepted my mother's death and also repented for my discontent with God, that I was "whole." However, I didn't realize that my psyche needed to also undergo healing. The experience of losing my mother was traumatizing. Having to visually watch my mother slowly die over the course of a few months (weight loss, physical disablement, medications, hospital admittance etc.) left severe wounds on my mind. This in addition to other heart wrenching events that followed immediately after her death. The memories were like scenes from a movie that continued to painfully play over and over again in my mind no matter how hard I tried to turn it off. It was eating away at my thoughts and my spirit. My mind was in an immediate need of being made whole.

During this moment of revelation, the Lord was showing me that every component of my being needed to be fully healed. For every area of my being had been wounded by death and grief in some way. These areas being my mind, heart and spirit. And also, even physically. For at one point, I struggled with eating and weight loss. Losing approximately 8lbs or so. I was beginning to understand that as humans every component of our wellbeing is intrinsically intertwined and dependent on the other. If one area is lacking or suffering, it directly affects another component.

So, with the revelation God had given me, I accepted the message and knew that it was now time to humbly seek His face for comfort and direction.

I needed to be made whole.

Holistic Healing

It's never too late to pray.

As a child I remember hearing my grandmother make that statement. It wasn't until years later that I understood the meaning.

Regardless of where we may be in life or what events may have transpired, prayer is always applicable. Prayers have no expiration date, nor are they subject to becoming void. It's our permanent lifeline to God.

So, although my mind and spirit were still wounded from the trauma and voids that initially took place years prior, the power of prayer was still more than capable of healing and reversing the damage that was caused. For prayer is an invitation that gives the Lord access to personally touch, speak, heal, provide, teach and guide us during our greatest moments as well as our lowest. It is a platform that allows us to have a personal meeting with God although we cannot see Him with the physical eye. Having faith enough to know that upon hearing even the faintest cry or whisper, that He'll willingly grace us with His presence and touch us in a way that supersedes any physical encounter we could ever have.

I needed to be touched.
I needed to be healed.
I needed to fervently pray.

Lord, heal my mind….
As I prayed, I wasn't exactly sure on what to say. So, in a childlike way I simply repeated this phrase over and over.

Lord, heal my mind….
Lord, heal my mind….

Although I had an active and consistent prayer life, I felt as though I was entering into a realm of prayer that I had never entered into before. Most of my prayers, regarding my personal wellbeing, were centered on thanking God for the gift of life and asking Him to cover and protect me from danger and harm. Along with asking Him to give me wisdom and strength from day to day. But with the current circumstances my request and focus were for my mental health and psyche. Issues that were extremely deep, intimate and painful.

Concerns and matters that typically weren't included in my everyday prayers. But the Lord had made it very clear to me that it was time to address and begin to heal in these areas. To be honest, to an extent I thought it was only natural to have these pains that I carried. Like a soldier that had been wounded in battle, I considered my mental woes to simply be a consequence of war. Scars and injuries that I would just have to manage to live with after suffering such a great loss.

However, this isn't true.

With the help of God, it was more than possible to be fully and not just partially healed from the inside out. Spiritually, emotionally and mentally. And the Lord was showing me this.

Lord …

In plain terms, I began to tell the Lord about the memories that were painfully ingrained in my mind and the void that was like a hole in my spirit. As I knew I could, I began to talk to the Lord as my friend.

Lord, I feel like I'm always missing something...

Lord, my mind is traumatized from seeing my mother lose weight and become disabled. It's still so painful to think about.

Lord, it's like I can still hear the hospital machines beeping and ringing in my ears...

It messed me up seeing and knowing she died in our home… Lord, I just...

It wasn't long before my face and hands were covered in tears as I poured my pain out to God. Painful images and memories from almost ten years ago began to flood my mind. At times there were more tears than words. But even still I knew the Lord understood. So, I kept crying, and I kept praying. I knew and could feel within my spirit that a painful, yet necessary cleansing was taking place.

Without reserve I began to call out and identify different things one by one as they came to my mind. I wanted to cover all bases.

Lord I know there are some things I mentally blocked out and suppressed. Help me God. I need to remember so I can fully heal. No matter how painful, I need to remember.

And as I continued to pray honestly and openly, the Lord began to guide me deeper into prayer. I began to pray for **holistic healing.** I wasn't exactly sure what the term/concept meant although I had an idea, but it was God that placed it into my spirit as I was praying. So, in obedience I added it to my prayer.

Lord I pray for holistic healing in the name of Jesus.

This time of prayer was only one out of many that I continued to have as time went on. It would take more than just one single time of fervent prayer before I was made whole and secure in every area of my wellbeing. And I was okay with that. I understood that deep matters like this took time and consistency. Consistency in prayer and consistency in drawing closer and closer to God. But I knew of a certainty it would happen.

For just as it takes time for the darkness of the night sky to fully dissipate against the prevalent rays of the morning sun, I knew that in due time my morning would come.

And God was preparing me to see it.

*"For ye see your calling, brethren, how that not many wise men
after the flesh, not many mighty, not many noble, are called:
But God hath chosen the foolish things of the world to confound
the wise; and God hath chosen the weak things of the world to
confound the things which are mighty;
And base things of the world, and things which are despised,
hath God chosen, yea, and things which are not, to bring to
nought things that are:
That no flesh should glory in his presence.
But of him are ye in Christ Jesus, who of God is made unto us
wisdom, and righteousness, and sanctification, and redemption."*
– I Corinthians 1:26-30

An Immediate Need

Holistic-
*To comprehend the parts of something as being interconnected and
as a whole. To support and treat the whole person taking into account
their physical, mental, emotional and spiritual wellbeing.*

*An approach that focuses on the overall wellbeing and not only the
person's illness or condition.*

I took the time to research the term that the Lord had revealed
to me.

Holistic.

Once I had taken the time to read and understand the
definition and concept, it made perfect sense as to why the Lord
laid it upon my spirit to pray for. In addition to this, it was also

amazing to see how the Lord stepped into the role of becoming like that of a teacher to me. Opening my mind and teaching me terms and concepts that were unfamiliar to me. Once again proving how vast, compassionate, and amazing He was.

The Lord took the time to not only educate me by revealing truths in the natural and spiritual, but also He began to show and teach me about my personal identity in Him. In other words, who and what He was calling me to be. There were some areas of my identity and calling that were obvious as I continued to operate and serve God in various ministries and roles within my church and also interact with people in my everyday life. However, I wasn't fully aware of another calling He had placed upon me. In my mind, I wasn't qualified to serve in this capacity due to my own hardships and struggles. It didn't seem fathomable. However, God in His perfect wisdom, was allowing those same hardships to become a resource that would allow me to connect and intimately relate to an audience of people that I was still currently a part of myself during this time.

For although I was oblivious to it, there was an immediate need. And with each day and moment that passed by, bit by bit, the Lord was grooming me to fulfill it.

Of a surety, I would soon realize that what I personally considered an automatic disqualification, was in fact a mandatory prerequisite for the need and the calling.

"Arise, shine; for thy light is come, and the glory of the LORD is risen upon thee."
– Isaiah 60:1

A Sixth Sense

They're overwhelmed with grief. I know they are. They never act that way.
They're battling depression. It's all over them.
They're quiet, but their body language is saying everything.
You can see it in their eyes. They're extremely hurt and broken.

Beyond just mere observation, I had developed what could be considered a sixth sense regarding being able to identify the signs of grief in the lives of those around me. Even people I only remotely knew. Initially, I assumed that I was over generalizing and or biasedly comparing my personal experiences with the experiences of others. In other words, reading deeper into a situation than what was necessary. But this wasn't the case. As if overnight, God had literally opened my eyes and had developed within me a spiritual intuition to inadeptly discern the pains and burdens of those around me that were mourning. Causing me to become extremely sensitive to their woes even without always fully knowing the exact details of their situation. I could simply *feel* it. Involuntarily, their burden had become *my* burden. Becoming unshakable to the point that no matter how much I tried to divert and separate my mind and feelings from it, the compassion I felt instead only deepened. Week after week, my thoughts were consumed with concern for those that I knew that had lost loved ones. Different people, different situations, different losses, various ages, but they all stayed on my mind and heart.

I was concerned as to how they were handling their grief. While also wondering whether they had a stable support system of family and friends that understood their plight. These individuals stayed on my prayer list just as much as they stayed on my mind.

The compassion I felt was definitely genuine, but I needed to know for certain that God was leading me to carry their burdens and that I wasn't just simply "feeling sorry" for people.

I needed clarity.

Lord, is this you?

Thankfully God in His perfect ways provided me with confirmation and removed all my doubts. To provide me with reassurance of this new burden and compassion that I carried, the Lord began to deal with and speak to me in dreams. While asleep at night the Lord began to show me vivid dreams of family members and friends that were in distress due to grief and loss. And as each dream unfolded, the Lord allowed me to see the pain and agony that my loved ones were suffering through. Allowing me to stand right in the midst of it all as everything took place. At times what I saw was startling and unsettling to see, yet I understood that there was a purpose behind it. The great detail that the Lord allowed me to see in the dreams was astounding. They weren't your ordinary dreams. To provide a glimpse as to what I saw, in these dreams I would see my loved ones weeping and distraught. Hunched over in pain. I was able to see and identify many different things: The clothes they wore, the place/ room they were in, the weather, the conversations, and the tears that covered their face. So much detail! Sometimes they were surrounded by a group of people and at other times they were completely alone. When looking at their faces I could see the despair and hopelessness in their eyes as they sat trying to figure out how to continue living their life without their loved one. It was obvious from their body language and it could be heard in their voices that they were desperate to have peace. But it was obvious that they were unsure of where and how to find it.

This was only one form of the dreams that the Lord allowed me to see. In other dreams, I would see my loved ones in extremely dangerous and compromising situations and environments. Sometimes absentmindedly sitting and staring off into the distance while being completely oblivious to the danger they were in. Sitting in an environment that was detrimental either physically, mentally, or spiritually. Sometimes a combination of all three. I would witness my loved ones partake in dangerous activities. Tears pouring down their face as they continued in the dangerous behavior and wallowed in their grief. Desperate to figure out how to cope with the pain of the loss. And in other forms of dreams, I would see my loved ones partaking in their normal everyday activities. Day to day activities like that of work, family life, church, etc. Yet as they moved along throughout their day, spontaneously their faces and extremities would begin to cave in and deteriorate. Literally pieces of their bodies would melt and fall off uncontrollably. However, despite the physical deterioration, they would continue to make an effort to have an ordinary day, but it was to no avail. It was clear that the physical deformity, which was a subliminal representation of their grief, was impeding their work and hindering them from accomplishing their everyday tasks.

So many dreams and so many different messages!

Each dream was significant in its own way in relation to the individual person. Every dream contained and presented an important message that was pertinent to not only the person of focus in the dream, but also it taught a lesson about the absolute truths of grief that was applicable to anyone in general.

Once I awoke, I would replay the dream in my mind over and over. Reflecting and asking God for help and direction as I analyzed the truths that were presented in the dream. Taking the time to write and compile a list of the messages that were being revealed.

1. God loves and has compassion on those that are mourning. He sees and understands exactly where we are physically, mentally and spiritually while grieving. His intent is not to abandon us, but to create a way to guide us to Him for comfort.

2. Grief is a universal experience. Every person, regardless of their walk in life, will encounter grief in some way. It's inevitable.

3. After suffering a loss, we as people look for a means to cope and restabilize our hearts and minds. There are many options, but not every option is rational and or appropriate. We have to be able to soberly distinguish the options that are healthy from the ones that are harmful.

4. Those around us that are on the outside looking in may be able to see potential and explicit danger that we're blind to because of grief. The environment that we're in and the people that we're around may not be conducive to our healing.

5. Although a person may continue to live and partake in their everyday activities after losing a loved one, this doesn't necessarily signify that they've overcome the pains of grief. Outwardly they may appear to be perfectly fine, yet over time any unresolved and hidden pains will become undeniably evident. Becoming a hindrance to their livelihood, relationships with people and deteriorating their health (mental/physical).

With a surety I knew that the Lord was allowing me to see and have these dreams in order for me to reach out and comfort my loved ones that were hurting. However, I was uncertain as to how or when I should contact them and what I should exactly say.

Should I tell them the full dream or just specific parts?

Do I relay every critical detail or just the overall truth and message? What if they think I'm judging them?

What if they aren't ready to talk about it?

Am I myself even ready for this?

I had a million questions floating in my mind. But I had to come to terms and realize that I simply needed to trust God. I couldn't simply roll over and continue sleeping while those I loved continued to live day in and day out with no rest or peace of mind. I knew that the Lord wouldn't create a burden of compassion in me for those that are grieving in addition to giving me undeniable dreams, only to allow it all to backfire and not fulfill its purpose.

I had to speak up.

It was imperative that I obey God and not let my fear and insecurities interfere with the work God was doing.

I had to have faith that God would give me the words to say and provide wisdom on how to deal with each individual. Knowing that He would guide me as I relied on Him to lead.

So, in nervousness, I began to contact each person as I continued to have various dreams over the weeks and months that passed by. With every contact that was made, each individual would confirm and verify what I saw in the dream. Statements such as *Yes! That is exactly what happened!* and *I'm doing my best to get rid of this situation/behavior* were made. Each person, even if they were shocked and taken aback, was receptive to the messages of the dream. It was a relief to know that my fears didn't come true after so much worry and nervousness. At times relaying the dreams felt awkward, but as time passed I became more comfortable in doing so. It was no question at all that it was the Lord that was giving me the confidence and the strength to retell the message that was given to me and reach out to those in need.

From these encounters and experiences wholesome bonds were formed between myself and the person. Beautiful and unique friendships. The initial discussions, regarding the dreams, transformed into unforgettable heartfelt moments of transparency and empathy. Moments that consisted of both them and I openly discussing where we were in our personal journeys. Discussing our times of joy, times of pain, our personal perception of life and death, our strength and weaknesses, and our relationship with God. These moments were just as uplifting and beneficial for myself as it was for them.

For although I still missed my mother greatly, I now had an indescribable fulfillment that I now felt and carried on the inside. A fulfillment that only came about from first experiencing pain and loss and in time also first-handedly experiencing the embrace and love of God *after* the loss. I could personally speak and advocate for both sides. And it was only by the help and grace of God that I was now able to rise and meet a need that at one point seemed unfathomable for my personal predicament.

Lord, this is completely you. Your hand is all over this.

I was completely blown away by the work God was doing right before my eyes.

I understood that every spoken word, personal touch, gift, and every other token of love was ultimately inspired by Him. I was just the vessel. And as a vessel, the more I poured out, the more God would pour into me. In other words, I never found myself empty as I continued to pour love into others. The void and brokenness that I carried for so long began to diminish as I surrendered myself to be led by God to help fill a need. In a way, it was as if by beckoning to the Lord's call, it filled my voids and became a balm to the wounds I never thought could fully heal. Fulfilling my purpose had undoubtedly brought about the healing I so desperately needed.

And regarding reaching out to others, the compassion I formed didn't simply stop with the dreams, but continued even further. As time went on, the Lord would place people on my heart at opportune times. Orchestrating the times perfectly for the circumstance at hand. Not only during their time of the initial loss, but other significant times such as the birth of a child, birthdays, holidays, the anniversary of the death, times of sickness and overall any significant time consolation was needed. It's amazing as to how delicate and sensitive the Lord is with His people.

And to further verify this truth about God's character, the scriptures teach us about the love and comfort of God. The Word states that God comforts us so that in turn we can also comfort others at the appropriate time.

"Blessed be God, even the Father of our Lord Jesus Christ,
the Father of mercies, and the God of all comfort;
Who comforteth us in all our tribulation, that we may
be able to comfort them which are in any trouble, by the
comfort wherewith we ourselves are comforted of God."
– I Corinthians 1:3-4

God alone is the greatest source of mercy and comfort. Being both the creator and provider of each. The scripture teaches us that He is more than capable of addressing and effectively meeting every need that we may have when hurting and or in distress. Which is why He is referred to as the God of **all** comfort. For although hardships and tribulations are unwanted, the scriptures let us know that God is present with us during these difficult times. The Lord doesn't abandon or neglect us, but instead comes to our aid when we need Him most.

The comfort He freely gives us not only brings healing to us personally, but also dually operates as a tool that prepares and spiritually grooms us to take on the burdens of others. "... *that we may be able to comfort them which are in any trouble,"*

Proving that spiritual growth and ministry (servanthood) is the intended result that God desires out of us. Overall, although the tribulations we experience are grievous at first, it ultimately is a beautiful process that's being used to draw us closer to God and to one another in love.

That's the entire purpose.

And just like that, it dawned on me.

I realized that our night experiences shouldn't be despised or disregarded, but instead fully embraced. There was more to the night than just sorrow. For God not only created the morning, but He *also* created the night. Each has a divine purpose and plays a significant role in our spiritual wellbeing.

Why couldn't I see this before?

It was as if my eyes had finally adjusted to see the truth that was before me the entire time.

Night was just as brilliant and beautiful as the morning.

"And God said, Let there be light: and there was light.
And God saw the light, that it was good: and God divided
the light from the darkness. And God called the light Day,
and the darkness he called Night. And the evening and the
morning were the first day."
– Genesis 1:3-5

Night Vision

Before there was light, darkness existed alone. And unlike the common and typical perception of darkness, initially darkness at the beginning of creation represented wonder and opportunity. In the hands of God, it was a viable platform that allowed the Lord to showcase His genius and His power.

The Word states *"And God said, Let there be light: and there was light."* By God simply speaking, light was produced out of the darkness. And in continuation, the scriptures show us that not only light, but also every other part of creation came forth out of what was first simply darkness. When reading the Word, it would seem as though darkness was insignificant or unwanted due to the Lord seeing fit to create its complete opposite being light. But this isn't so. For the scripture states *"And God called the light Day, and the darkness he called Night."* Just as He gave the light a unique title, (Day) He also did the same for the darkness. (Night)

This signifying that both were intentionally designed by Him with a significant purpose. Also, it signified that each would play a key role in creation and in the lives of mankind. For although light and darkness were opposites, they were complements to one another and made a whole. Neither one is complete without the other. "*...And the evening and the morning were the first day,*" Genesis 1:5.

However, although they make one whole, there are distinct differences between the two. When initially created by God darkness and light were both divinely pure. This connotation has remained regarding light, however it has changed regarding darkness. After the fall of man and once sin entered into the world, darkness was used to signify death, evil, punishment, sadness, and even the absence of God.

While light, on the other hand, continued to represent purity, hope, life and the presence of God. The definition and dynamics have changed drastically since the beginning of creation. This can be seen in our personal lives and in our world today.

Any and every aspect or experience of human life that evokes feelings of pain, misery, evil or fear are directly associated with the concept of darkness and the night. It is our metaphorical resort when explaining critical and difficult times that we're experiencing in our life. To verify this truth, we see examples in the scriptures on this matter.

*"Let the day perish wherein I was born, and the night in which it was said, There is a man child conceived. Let that day be **darkness**; let not God regard it from above, neither let the light shine upon it. Let darkness and the shadow of death stain it; let a cloud dwell upon it; let the blackness of the day terrify it."*

– Job 3:3-5

"Let my prayer come before thee: incline thine ear unto my cry;
For my soul is full of troubles: and my life draweth nigh unto
the grave. I am counted with them that go down into the pit:
I am as a man that hath no strength: Free among the dead,
like the slain that lie in the grave, whom thou rememberest no
more: and they are cut off from thy hand. Thou hast laid me in
*the lowest pit, in **darkness**, in the deeps."*
– Psalm 88:2-6

Just from these two scriptures alone it is obvious that darkness has become the face of grief and misery. However, as we continue to read and study the scriptures we can see that darkness signifies and explains more than just human grievances. The Word of God shows us that darkness is a multifaceted concept that is used to help us more inadeptly understand the character of God. Listed below are subtopic points and scriptures that provide us with understanding about the purpose of darkness in connection to spiritual matters.

1. **Darkness is a moment and place where we can receive direct revelation from God.**

"And the people stood afar off, and Moses drew near unto
*the thick **darkness** where God was. And the LORD said unto*
Moses, Thus thou shalt say unto the children of Israel, Ye have
seen that I have talked with you from heaven."
– Exodus 20:21-22

*"Then was the secret revealed unto Daniel in a **night** vision. Then Daniel blessed the God of heaven. Daniel answered and said, Blessed be the name of God for ever and ever: for wisdom and might are his: And he changeth the times and the seasons: he removeth kings, and setteth up kings: he giveth wisdom unto the wise, and knowledge to them that know understanding: He revealeth the deep and secret things: he knoweth what is in the **darkness**, and the light dwelleth with him."*
– Daniel 2:19-22

2. **Darkness gives us the opportunity to self-reflect on our personal relationship with God.**

"But if thine eye be evil, thy whole body shall be full of darkness. If therefore the light that is in thee be darkness, how great is that darkness."
– Matthew 6:23

*"And now, behold, the hand of the Lord is upon thee, and thou shalt be blind, not seeing the sun for a season. And immediately there fell on him a mist and a **darkness**; and he went about seeking some to lead him by the hand."*
(Conversion of Saul)
– Acts 13:11

3. Darkness is used as a foreshadowing to reveal the Promises of God.

*"And when the sun was going down, a deep sleep fell upon Abram; and, lo, a horror of great **darkness** fell upon him. And he said unto Abram, Know of a surety that thy seed shall be a stranger in a land that is not theirs, and shall serve them; and they shall afflict them four hundred years; And also that nation, whom they shall serve, will I judge: and afterward shall they come out with great substance."*
– Genesis 15:12-14

*"And it was about the sixth hour, and there was a **darkness** over all the earth until the ninth hour. And the sun was **darkened**, and the veil of the temple was rent in the midst. And when Jesus had cried with a loud voice, he said, Father, into thy hands I commend my spirit: and having said thus, he gave up the ghost."*
– Luke 23:45-47

4. Darkness is used to represent sin and estrangement from God.

*"Such as sit in **darkness** and in the shadow of death, being bound in affliction and iron; Because they rebelled against the words of God, and contemned the counsel of the most High."*
– Psalm 107:10-11

*"This I say therefore, and testify in the Lord, that ye henceforth walk not as other Gentiles walk, in the vanity of their mind, having the understanding **darkened**, being alienated from the life of God through the ignorance that is in them, because of the blindness of their heart."*
– **Ephesians 4:17-18**

5. Darkness is used to represent hell and eternal damnation.

"And cast ye the unprofitable servant into outer darkness: there shall be weeping and gnashing of teeth."
– **Matthew 25:30**

Revelation, self-reflection, estrangement, the promises of God, and eternal damnation are just a few of possibly many more spiritual concepts that are represented by darkness. For just as it was during the time of Creation, darkness remains to be a platform for God to showcase His divine purpose and power. And although the stain of sin has altered its initial purity, even still God is able to use darkness in this particular aspect for His glory.

When we study the scriptures listed above within their context, every scripture blatantly shows us that darkness, and the matters of it, are completely subject to and under the hand of God just as it was in the beginning. For during Creation when God spoke the light into existence, the darkness shifted and submitted to the command of God so that the light could fully appear. This shows us that God has full authority over darkness AND the light. And regarding eternal damnation (hell), God has the authority to also disallow the light from being manifested at all. Once again, thus proving His Superiority.

These truths are also applicable to us as people regarding spiritual matters.

The darkness, and the moments thereof, serve a divine purpose and have intentionally been allowed by God to transpire in our lives. These moments are not only for a specific purpose, but also are for a set and distinct period of time according to the Lord's timing. Other than the possibility of eternal damnation, the dark and grievous moments we experience were never intended by God to be the conclusion to our life story. But instead, a catalyst for the light to appear. As said, a platform.

A platform for God to speak.
A platform for God to teach.
A platform for God to lead.
A platform for God to renew.
A platform for God to save.

And overall, a platform for the God of Light to execute an unforgettable performance in our life right before our eyes despite the darkness that surrounds us.

Allowing us to see and undoubtedly know that He is Lord over the light **and** the darkness.

"The day is thine, the night also is thine: thou hast prepared the light and the sun," Psalm 74:16.

So, although darkness, in the mind of man, may appear to be an uncontrollable and unsalvageable moment or time that places us beyond the realm and reach of God, it isn't. Instead, it is a moment and time that positions us directly within His reach. Giving us the opportunity to be closer to God than we have ever been before.

Letting us know and understand that He exists in the darkness just as well as He does in the light. For it is in the darkness that we are able to come face to face with God and fully *see* who God is.

In summary, although the grief we endure may seem unbearable, by choosing to draw nigh unto God during the night, joy is a guaranteed promise to us.

"...in his favour is life: weeping may endure for a night, but joy cometh in the morning," *Psalm 30:5.*

For He is our comfort during the night and our reason for joy in the morning.

Healing.
Revelation.
Surrenderance.
Purpose.
Joy.

My morning had finally come.

*"For God who commanded the light to shine out of
darkness, hath shined in our hearts, to give the light of the
knowledge of the glory of God in the face of Jesus Christ."*
– II Corinthians 4:6

The Morning After Mourning

"Look Mommy! The sun is here!"
At three years old my daughter is always enthused to see the sun rising in the sky in the morning. She anxiously looks and points at the blinds letting me know that she can see *"yellow"* coming into the room. Without question, she reminds me of myself. Reminding me of the child I once was and the adult I currently am. I'm older in age, but my love for the sun and the beauty of it still remains. However, I now view the sun and the morning in a different light. Looking back and reflecting on my life over the last eleven years, I undoubtedly know and understand God's Divine purpose for the challenges I faced: He was creating a light within me. A light, that unlike the morning sun, is unable to fall prey to looming clouds, overwhelming fog, relentless storms, and or darkness in its deepest form. A light that never sets, but instead continues to rise.

At the onset of my personal daybreak, just as my mourning was exchanged for the morning, my sun was exchanged for the Son. This of course being Jesus Christ our Savior and light of the world. *(John 8:12)*

For it is by and through him that every form of grievous darkness is destroyed and dually the light of God is fully manifested to man. *(I Timothy 1:1)(Matthew 4:16–17)(Acts 26:15–18)*

Although I initially received salvation through Jesus Christ prior to my mother's death, it wasn't until I faced my darkest moment that I obtained a greater understanding regarding the life and ministry of Jesus Christ and the light of life that lived within him.

As a child, I received and understood him to be the means by which our souls were saved. (Acts 2:21,32-38) Yet, I still had to learn the full purpose of the light of Christ that was within me as a born again believer. With the loss of my mother and the life events that transpired thereafter, my walk with Christ matured and extended beyond simply having the light, the Holy Ghost, living within me. It was during this time that I began to understand the purpose and power of the light of Christ.

The light was designed to not only represent the presence of God, but in addition it operates as a force that is more powerful than death itself. For the light of life that comes through Christ is *eternal.* In other words, no opposing force regardless of how great it is can cause it to come to an end or be destroyed.

> *"And I give unto them eternal life; and they shall never perish,*
> *neither shall any man pluck them out of my hand."*
> – John 10:28

As born again believers we have no reason to fear death or the deadly mechanisms of this world. And in addition to living in the world, although we must undergo tribulations, when we possess eternal life, we have full assurance that we will overcome any and all hardships that we encounter. Fully overcoming with the power of Christ and not that of our own.

"... My grace is sufficient for thee: for my strength is made perfect in weakness. Most gladly therefore will I rather glory in my infirmities, that the power of Christ may rest upon me."
– II Corinthians 12:9

"Who is he that overcometh the world, but he that believeth that Jesus is the Son of God?"
– I John 5:5

"Jesus said unto her, I am the resurrection, and the life: he that believeth in me, though he were dead, yet shall he live:" "And whosoever liveth and believeth in me shall never die. Believest thou this?"
– John 11:25-26

Despite the suffering, persecution, and or earthly loss that we face, it can never triumph over the gift of eternal life that we receive when we receive the spirit of Christ. For even in death, just like Christ, the power of eternal life is what causes us to live forever even after we personally experience death and leave the earth. Ultimately making our final home with the Lord in heaven.

So, although death and darkness carry the intimidating image of misery and fear, it is powerless when compared to the image and light of Christ.

For every morning the Son rises.

Conclusion

As the years have passed by, such as it is in life, I have continued to say goodbye to loved ones as they have transitioned from life here on earth. And in contrast to how I initially viewed death during the passing of my mother and so many others that I loved, I can now say with full assurance that death gives life. Or rather, the opportunity for a *true life* to begin. This being a life beyond a mere heartbeat, a functioning mind, and physical mobility. For these things can perish at any moment whether separately or simultaneously. However, in this context, I'm referring to life regarding those of us that are living intentionally taking every opportunity in **this** life to create, build, sow, renew, and permanently establish a positive legacy not only for the sake of ourselves, but for others also. Becoming self-driven and willing to learn, change, grow, remove or add to the life that we're currently living. In other words, creating a life that gives life to others even after our time on earth has ended. For experiencing death second handedly allows us to clearly see that not only are we accountable to make a decision regarding our souls, but also it presents the opportunity for us to self-reflect and ask ourselves the question *"Once my finally breath has been taken, will my words, love, wisdom, character, choices, and overall **life**, breathe life into somebody else?"* Only each of us individually can control and determine this outcome.

Friends and family, in honesty we must ask ourselves, will my death **give** life?

In regards to my mother's life I am extremely grateful to say that she in fact created and established a legacy that gave the gift of life even after her death. Not just for myself as her daughter, but so many others as well.

Our lives don't have to end once our eyes close, nor does it have to be confined to the burial site that we are placed in. For with the power and life of Christ and self-determination, it is simply formed and transitioned into a new one.

For truth be told, **true life** never ends.

Good Morning
To the child that lost a parent, Good Morning.

To the mother that had to bury her son,
Good Morning.

To the father that misses his daughter,
Good Morning.

To the parents that long to hear their infant's cry,
 Good Morning.

To the spouse that's battling loneliness,
Good Morning.

To the nurse that had to make the final call,
Good Morning.

To the paramedic that desperately tried,
Good Morning.

To the grandchild that misses their grandparent,
Good Morning.

To the grandparent that's mourning their grandchild,
Good Morning.

To the believer who's seeking God, Good Morning.

To the silent griever, Good Morning.

To the outlandish griever, Good Morning.

To the sibling that's consumed in grief, Good Morning.

To the relative that *"didn't see it coming"*...
Good Morning.

To the best friend that feels friendless, Good Morning.

To the Pastor that needs consoling too, Good Morning.

And to the believer that died in the faith, Absolutely, Good Morning.

To all, I say Good Morning.

"...weeping may endure for a night, but joy cometh in the morning."
– Psalm 30:5

The Morning After Mourning

www.ingramcontent.com/pod-product-compliance
Lightning Source LLC
Chambersburg PA
CBHW021218130726
47988CB00002B/712